PHILIP'S JUNIOR SCHOOL ATLAS

Philip's World Atlases are published in association with The Royal Geographical Society (with The Institute of British Geographers).

The Society was founded in 1830 and given a Royal Charter in 1859 for 'the advancement of geographical science'. Today it is a leading world centre for geographical learning – supporting education, teaching, research and expeditions, and promoting public understanding of the subject.

Further information about the Society and how to join may be found on its website at: **www.rgs.org**

Published in Great Britain by Philip's, a division of Octopus Publishing Group Limited (www.octopusbooks.co.uk) Endeavour House, 189 Shaftesbury Avenue, London WC2H 8JY An Hachette UK Company (www.hachette.co.uk)

Cartography by Philip's

Ordnance Survey® Page 2 Bath city map (top right): This product includes mapping licensed from Ordnance Survey® with the permission of the Controller of Her Majesty's Stationery Office. © Crown copyright 2006. All rights reserved. Licence number 100011710.

© 1993, 2011 Philip's
First published 1993
Second edition 1997
Third edition 1999
Fourth edition 2003
Fifth edition 2006
Sixth edition 2008
Seventh edition 2011

A CIP catalogue record for this book is available from the British Library.

ISBN 978-1-84907-168-0 (HARDBACK EDITION)
ISBN 978-1-84907-169-7 (PAPERBACK EDITION)

Printed in Hong Kong

Details of other Philip's titles and services can be found on our website at: **www.philips-maps.co.uk**

What is a map?

These small maps explain the meaning of some of the lines and colours on the atlas maps.

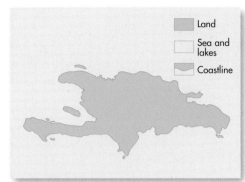

1. Land and sea This is how an island is shown on a map. The land is coloured green and the sea is blue. The coastline is a blue line.

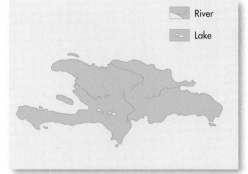

2. Rivers and lakes There are some lakes on the island and rivers that flow down to the sea.

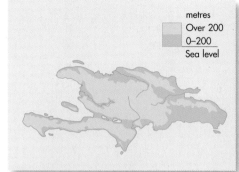

3. Height of the land – 1 This map shows the land over 200 metres high in a lighter colour. The height of the land is shown by contour lines and layer colours.

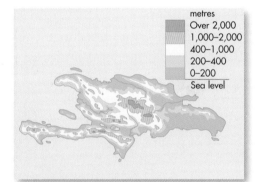

4. Height of the land – 2 This map shows more contour lines and layer colours. It shows that the highest land is in the centre of the island and that it is over 2,000 metres high.

5. Countries This is a way of showing different information about the island. It shows that the island is divided into two countries. They are separated by a country boundary.

6. Cities and towns There are cities and towns on the island. The two capital cities are shown with a special symbol. Other large or important cities are also shown by a red square or circle.

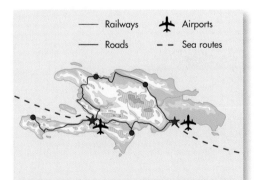

7. Transport information This map shows the most important roads, railways, airports and sea routes. Transport routes connect the cities and towns.

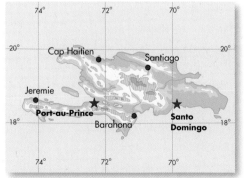

8. Where is the island? This map gives the lines of latitude and longitude and shows where the island is in the world. Page 59 in the atlas shows the same island at a different scale.

9. A complete map – using the country colouring and showing the letter-figure codes used in the index.

1

Scale

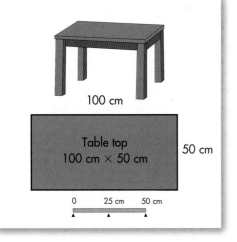

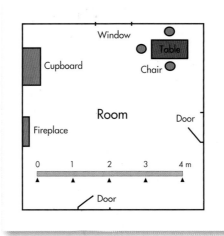

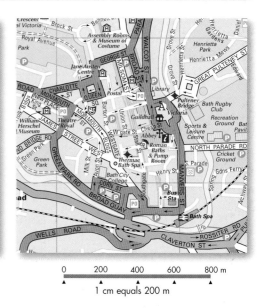

This is a drawing of the top of a table, looking down on it. It is 100 cm wide and 50 cm from front to back. The drawing measures 4 × 2 cm. It is drawn to scale: 1 cm on the drawing equals 25 cm on the table.

This is a plan of a room looking down from above. 1 cm on the map equals 1 metre in the room. The same table is shown, but now at a smaller scale. Use the scale bar to find the measurements of other parts of the room.

This is a map of an area in the city of Bath. Large buildings can be seen but other buildings are too small to show. Below are atlas maps of different scales.

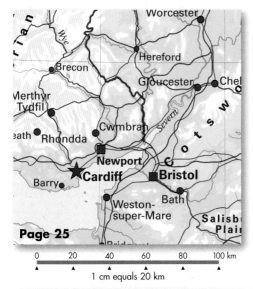

Page 25

0   20   40   60   80   100 km
1 cm equals 20 km

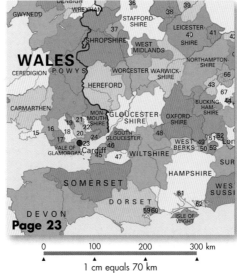

Page 23

0   100   200   300 km
1 cm equals 70 km

Page 50

0   300   600 km
1 cm equals 150 km

Scale bars

This distance represents 1 mile

This distance represents 1 kilometre

These examples of scale bars are at the scale of 1 cm equals 0.5 km

Signposts still have miles on them. 1 mile = 1.6 km, or 10 miles is the same as 16 kilometres. On maps of continents in this atlas, both a kilometre and a mile scale bar are shown.

On the maps of the continents, where you cannot see the British Isles, a small map of the British Isles is shown. It gives you some idea of size and scale.

BRITISH ISLES
On same scale

Direction

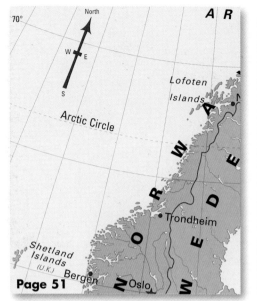

Page 51

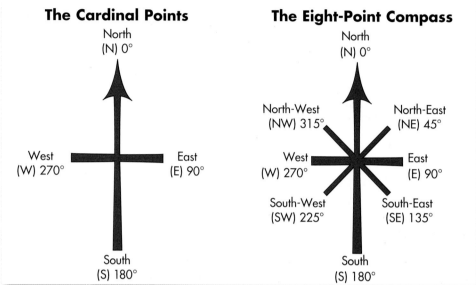

The Cardinal Points

North
(N) 0°

West
(W) 270°

East
(E) 90°

South
(S) 180°

The Eight-Point Compass

North
(N) 0°

North-West
(NW) 315°

North-East
(NE) 45°

West
(W) 270°

East
(E) 90°

South-West
(SW) 225°

South-East
(SE) 135°

South
(S) 180°

Many of the maps in this atlas have a North Point showing the direction of north. It points in the same direction as the lines of longitude. The four main directions shown are called the cardinal points.

Direction is measured in degrees. This diagram shows the degree numbers for each cardinal point. The direction is measured clockwise from north. The diagram on the right shows all the points of the compass and the divisions between the cardinal points. For example, between north and east there is north-east, between south and west is south-west. You can work out the cardinal points at your home by looking for the sun rising in the east and setting in the west.

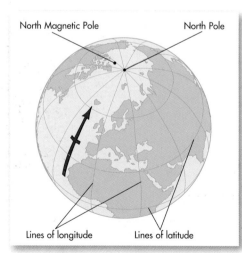

North Magnetic Pole

North Pole

Lines of longitude

Lines of latitude

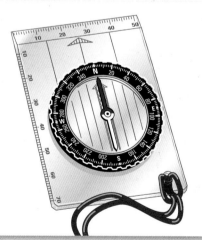

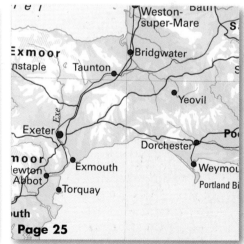

Page 25

The Earth has a spot near the North Pole that is called the Magnetic Pole. If a piece of metal that was magnetized at one end was left to float, then the magnetized tip would point to the North Magnetic Pole.

The needle of a compass is magnetized and it always points north. If you know where you are and want to go to another place, you can measure your direction from a map and use a compass to guide you.

This is part of map 25. North is at the top. Look at the points of the compass on the diagram above and the positions of places on the map. Taunton is north-east of Exeter and Dorchester is south-east of Taunton.

Latitude and longitude

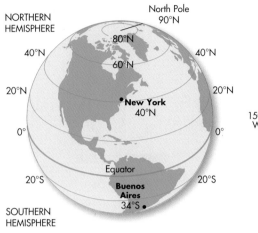

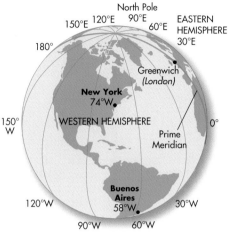

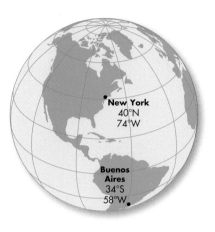

Latitude

This map shows part of the Earth seen from thousands of kilometres above New York. The Equator is exactly halfway between the North and South Poles. It divides the Earth into two hemispheres. The Equator is shown as a line on maps. It is numbered 0°. There are other lines on maps north and south of the Equator. They are called lines of latitude.

Longitude

Maps have another set of lines running north to south linking the Poles. These lines are called lines of longitude. The line numbered 0° runs through Greenwich in London, England, and is called the Prime Meridian. The other lines of longitude are numbered up to 180° east and west of 0°. Longitude line 180° runs through the Pacific Ocean.

Map references

The latitude and longitude lines on maps form a grid. In this atlas, the grid lines are in blue, and on most maps are shown for every ten degrees. The numbers of the lines can be used to give a reference to show the location of a place on a map. The index in this atlas uses another way of finding places. It lists the rows of latitude as numbers and the columns of longitude as letters.

Line of latitude with its number in degrees
Line of longitude with its number in degrees
Row number used in the index
Column letter used in the index

	Latitude	Longitude	Map page	Map letter-figure
Cairo, Africa	30°N	31°E	55	F2
Mexico City, N. America	19°N	99°W	59	H7
Mumbai, Asia	18°N	72°E	53	H7
Moscow, Europe	55°N	37°E	51	Q4
Sao Paulo, S. America	24°S	48°W	61	F6
Sydney, Oceania	34°S	151°E	57	F11

This table shows the largest city in each continent with its latitude and longitude. Look for them on the maps in this atlas.

Map information

Page 17

△ A map symbol shows the position of something – for example, circles for towns or an aeroplane for an airport.

Page 37

△ On some maps a dot or a symbol stands for a large number – for example, ten million people or two million tonnes of wheat or potatoes.

Page 19

△ The size of the symbol can be bigger or smaller, to show different numbers. The symbol here shows tourists.

Page 51

△ Colours are used on some maps so that separate areas, such as countries, as in this map, can be seen clearly.

Page 34

△ Patterns on maps often spread across country borders. This map shows different types of vegetation in the world.

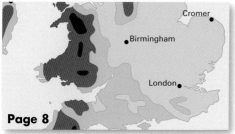

Page 8

△ On other maps, areas that are the same in some way have the same colour to show patterns. This map shows rainfall.

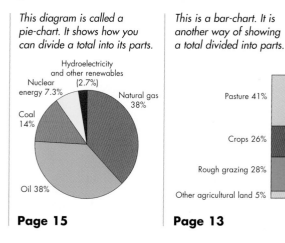

Page 36

△ Colours that are lighter or darker are used on some maps to show less or more of something. This map shows farming.

Graphs and charts

Graphs and charts are used to give more information about subjects shown on the maps. A graph shows how something changes over time.

This graph shows the rainfall for each month in a year as a blue bar that can be measured on the scale at the side of the graph.

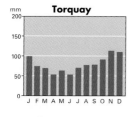

Page 8

This diagram is called a pie-chart. It shows how you can divide a total into its parts.

Hydroelectricity and other renewables (2.7%)
Nuclear energy 7.3%
Natural gas 38%
Coal 14%
Oil 38%

Page 15

This is a bar-chart. It is another way of showing a total divided into parts.

Pasture 41%
Crops 26%
Rough grazing 28%
Other agricultural land 5%

Page 13

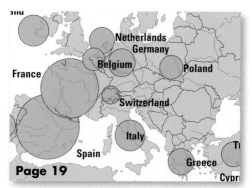

5

Rocks, mountains and rivers

Rocks

This map shows the different types of rock in Great Britain and Ireland.

Scale
0   200 km

Type of rock

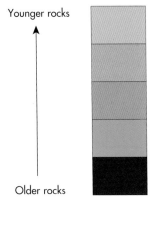

Younger rocks

Young sand, clay and river mud

Chalk

Sandstone, clay and young limestone
The limestone part

Old hard rocks, limestone, grit, coal, slate, shale and old sandstone

Very old hard rocks

Older rocks

Old volcanoes, granite and basalt

Glaciers came as far south as this line up to 10,000 years ago

Longest rivers

(length in kilometres)

Shannon	370
Severn	354
Thames	335
Trent	297
Aire	259
Ouse	230
Wye	215
Tay	188
Nene	161
Clyde	158

Largest islands

(square kilometres)

Great Britain	229,880
Ireland	84,400
Lewis and Harris	2,225
Skye	1,666
Shetland (Mainland)	967
Mull	899
Anglesey	714
Islay	615
Isle of Man	572
Isle of Wight	381

Largest lakes

(square kilometres)

Lough Neagh	382
Lough Corrib	168
Lough Derg	120
Lower Lough Erne	105
Loch Lomond	71
Loch Ness	57

The largest lake in England is Lake Windermere (15 square kilometres). The largest lake in Wales is Lake Vyrnwy (8 square kilometres).

Highest mountains

(height in metres)

In Scotland:
  Ben Nevis 1,344
In Wales:
  Snowdon 1,085
In Ireland:
  Carrauntoohill 1,041
In England:
  Scafell Pike 978
In Northern Ireland:
  Slieve Donard 852

Scale
0   200 km

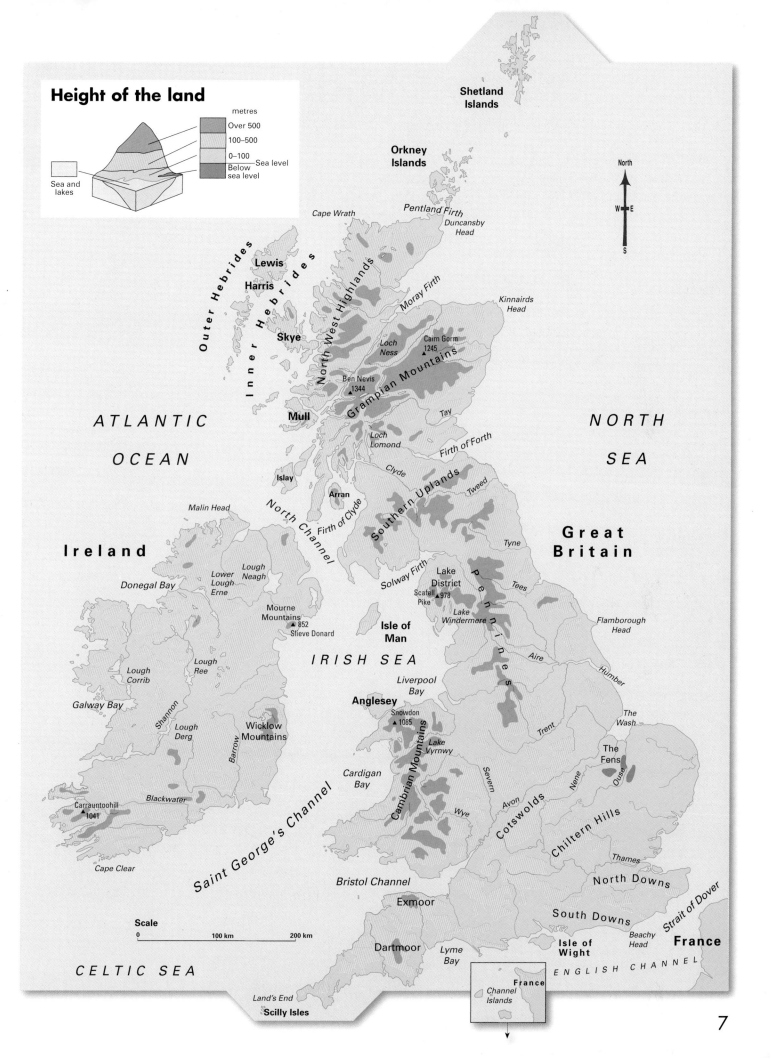

Height of the land

metres
Over 500
100–500
0–100
Sea level
Below sea level

Sea and lakes

North
W E
S

Shetland Islands

Orkney Islands

Cape Wrath

Pentland Firth

Duncansby Head

Outer Hebrides

Lewis

Harris

Inner Hebrides

Skye

North West Highlands

Moray Firth

Kinnairds Head

Loch Ness

Cairn Gorm 1245

Grampian Mountains

Ben Nevis 1344

Mull

Tay

Loch Lomond

Firth of Forth

ATLANTIC OCEAN

Islay

Arran

Clyde

Southern Uplands

Tweed

NORTH SEA

Firth of Clyde

Malin Head

North Channel

Great Britain

Ireland

Lough Neagh

Tyne

Lower Lough Erne

Solway Firth

Lake District

Tees

Donegal Bay

Mourne Mountains

852 Slieve Donard

Scafell Pike 978

Pennines

Lake Windermere

Flamborough Head

Isle of Man

IRISH SEA

Aire

Humber

Lough Corrib

Lough Ree

Liverpool Bay

The Wash

Shannon

Galway Bay

Anglesey

Snowdon 1085

Trent

The Fens

Lough Derg

Wicklow Mountains

Lake Vyrnwy

Ouse

Barrow

Blackwater

Cambrian Mountains

Cardigan Bay

Severn

Avon

Nene

Chiltern Hills

Carrauntoohill 1041

Cotswolds

Wye

Saint George's Channel

Bristol Channel

Thames

North Downs

Cape Clear

Exmoor

South Downs

Beachy Head

Strait of Dover

France

Dartmoor

Lyme Bay

Isle of Wight

ENGLISH CHANNEL

CELTIC SEA

Scale

0   100 km   200 km

Land's End

Scilly Isles

France

Channel Islands

7

Weather and climate

Rainfall is measured at many places in the UK every day. Each year, all the measurements are put together and graphs are made, like the ones shown on this page. Experts in the weather use these measurements to find out the average amount of rainfall in the UK for each year. They can then show this on weather maps, like the map below. Graphs and maps are also made for average temperatures and other types of weather (see opposite page). These help the experts to see patterns in the UK's weather over a long period of time. These patterns in the weather show a country's climate. The maps on these pages show you the climate of Great Britain and Ireland.

If you collect the rainfall each day and measure it, then you could draw a graph like this.

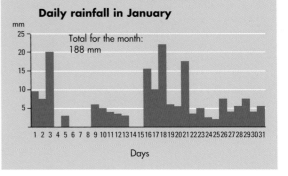

Daily rainfall in January

Total for the month: 188 mm

Rainfall

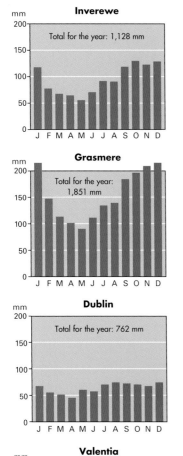

Inverewe
Total for the year: 1,128 mm

Grasmere
Total for the year: 1,851 mm

Dublin
Total for the year: 762 mm

Valentia
Total for the year: 1,400 mm

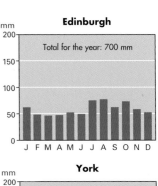

Amount of rain per year

millimetres
- Over 2,000
- 1,000–2,000
- 750–1,000
- Under 750
- Selected places with graphs round the map to show the amount of rain that falls each month

Highest average yearly rainfall: 5,000 mm (Sprinkling Tarn, in the Lake District)

Lowest average yearly rainfall: 500 mm (Isle of Grain)

Scale
0   200 km

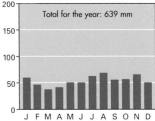

Edinburgh
Total for the year: 700 mm

York
Total for the year: 639 mm

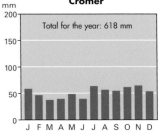

Cromer
Total for the year: 618 mm

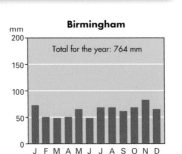

Torquay
Total for the year: 950 mm

Birmingham
Total for the year: 764 mm

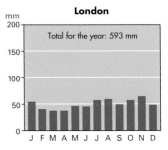

London
Total for the year: 593 mm

Wind

Stornoway
Tiree

Over 40 gales per year

Blacksod Point

Holyhead

Valentia

Tynemouth

London

Scilly Isles

Less than 20 gales per year

NW N NE
W E
SW S SE

100 days
50
0

*The bars show the number of days that the wind blows **from** the direction shown.*

Sun

Average number of hours of sunshine per day
- Over 5
- 4–5
- 3–4
- Under 3

Least sunny part of the British Isles

Sunniest part of the British Isles

Snow

Average number of mornings per year when snow is lying on the ground
- Over 50
- 20–50
- 10–20
- 5–10
- Under 5

Snow lying on average 55 mornings per year

Snow lying on average only 1 morning per year

Temperature

Birmingham — Average temperature for year: 10°C
Dublin — Average temperature for year: 10°C
Edinburgh — Average temperature for year: 9°C
London — Average temperature for year: 11°C
Plymouth — Average temperature for year: 11°C

(Months: J F M A M J J A S O N D; °C scale 0–20)

Winter temperature

Average temperature for January
- Over 6°C
- 4–6°C
- 2–4°C
- 0–2°C
- Under 0°C

Average daily temperature: 0°C
Lowest-ever recorded temperature: −27°C

Edinburgh
Dublin
Birmingham
London
Plymouth

Scale
0   200 km

Average daily temperature: 8°C

Summer temperature

Average temperature for July
- Over 16°C
- 14–16°C
- 12–14°C
- 10–12°C
- Under 10°C

Average daily temperature: 12°C

Edinburgh
Dublin
Birmingham
London
Plymouth

Scale
0   200 km

Average daily temperature: 17°C

Highest-ever recorded temperature: 38°C

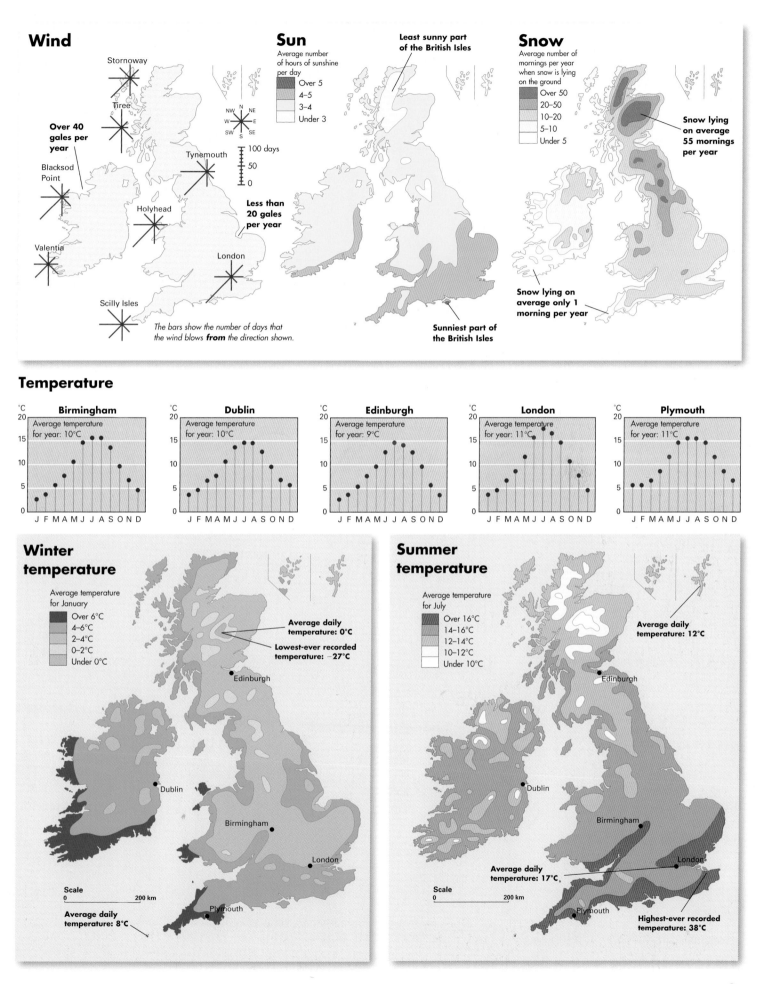

9

People, cities and towns

The UK Census

Every ten years, there is a government survey in the UK. The head of each household has to fill in a form. On the form, there are questions about the house and the people who live there. This is called the Census. The Census tells the government the number of people living in the UK. This helps the government to plan such things as schools and hospitals. The Census shows how the population has changed during the last century.

Here are some of the questions asked on the Census form:
How old are you?
Have you moved house in the last year?
In which country were you born?
To which ethnic group do you belong?
Have you a long-term illness?
Can you speak Welsh?
What do you do for a job?
How many hours a week do you work?
How do you get to work?
Where do you work?
Do you own or rent your house?
Do you have a bath, flush toilet or central heating?
Do you have a car?

People

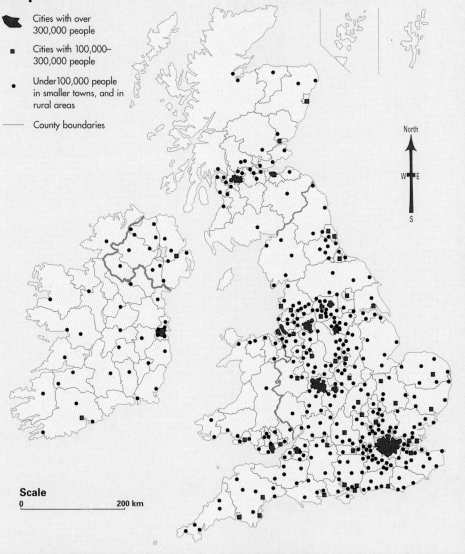

- Cities with over 300,000 people
- Cities with 100,000–300,000 people
- Under 100,000 people in smaller towns, and in rural areas
- County boundaries

North

Scale
0 ——————————— 200 km

Country population data

	1901	2001	2011
		millions	
England	30.5	49.2	52.5
Wales	2.0	2.9	3.0
Scotland	4.5	5.1	5.3
Northern Ireland	1.2	1.7	1.9
United Kingdom	**38.2**	**58.9**	**62.7**
Isle of Man	0.055	0.076	0.084
Channel Islands	0.096	0.147	0.157
Ireland	**3.2**	**3.9**	**4.7**

Changing numbers

United Kingdom

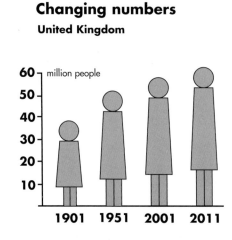

million people

60
50
40
30
20
10

1901 1951 2001 2011

Ireland

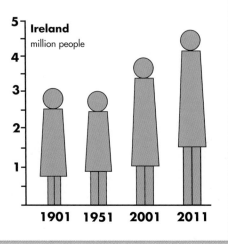

million people

5
4
3
2
1

1901 1951 2001 2011

Cities

Cities
- Cities with over 300,000 people
- Cities with 100,000–300,000 people

Population in 1991, 2001 and 2011

	1991	2001	2011
	thousand people		
London	6,890	7,188	7,200
Birmingham	1,007	976	992
Leeds	717	716	720
Glasgow	689	579	560
Sheffield	529	513	512
Edinburgh	440	449	450
Liverpool	481	439	440
Manchester	439	393	420
Bristol	397	392	380
Cardiff	294	308	310
Coventry	305	300	305
Nottingham	281	284	285
Leicester	285	287	280
Belfast	294	277	280
Sunderland	294	289	280
Hull	267	260	262
Newcastle	278	260	259
Plymouth	254	255	258
Stoke-on-Trent	253	254	239
Dublin	940	977	1,045
Cork	174	180	190

These are the largest cities in the UK and Ireland. Note that very few increased their populations between 1991 and 2011.

Scale
0 — 200 km

Young people

In these counties, young people are a large group in the population (over 20%). On this map young people are those aged under 15 years old.

In these counties, old people are a large group in the population (over 20%). On this map old people are women aged over 60 and men over 65 years old.

Look at these two maps. Can you think of some reasons why some counties have more older people than other counties?

Old people

Farming and fishing

Types of farm

Dairy farms
Cows for milk, butter and cheese

Beef farms
Cows and calves for beef and veal

Sheep farms
Sheep and lambs for wool and meat

Grain and root farms
Wheat, potatoes, sugar beet and oilseed rape

Mixed farms
Livestock and grain or roots

Market gardening
Vegetables, fruit and flowers

Forests

Big cities

The small maps show where different types of crops are grown.

North
W E
S

Scale
0   200 km

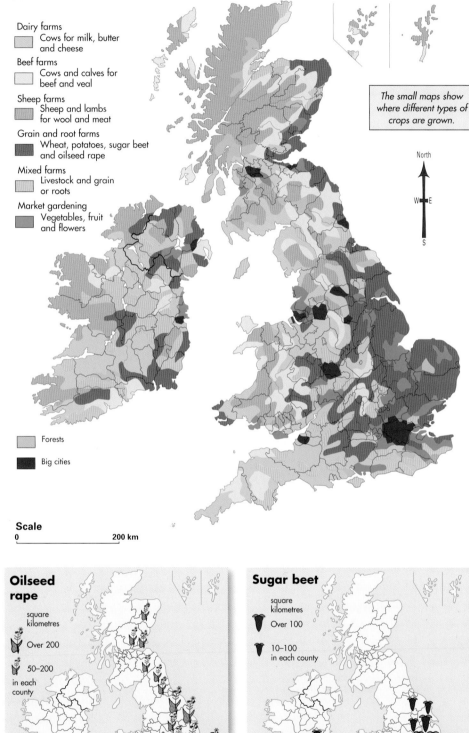

Wheat
square kilometres

Over 1,000

250–1,000 in each county

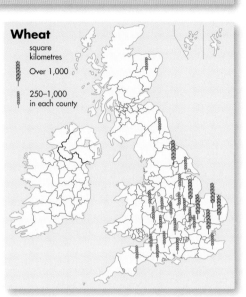

Potatoes
square kilometres

Over 100

25–100 in each county

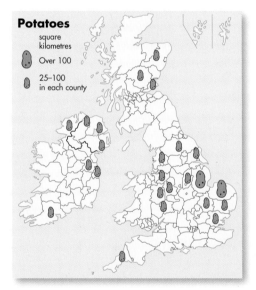

Oilseed rape
square kilometres

Over 200

50–200 in each county

Sugar beet
square kilometres

Over 100

10–100 in each county

Vegetables
square kilometres

Over 100

10–100 in each county

12

Cattle

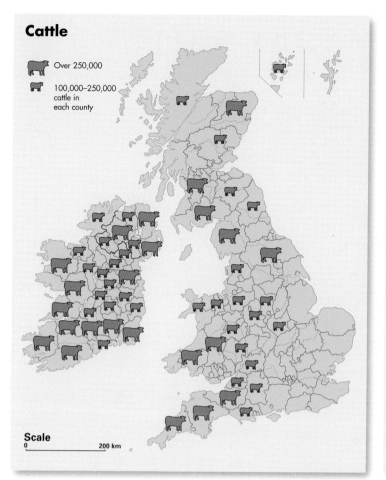

- Over 250,000
- 100,000–250,000 cattle in each county

Scale
0 — 200 km

Sheep and pigs

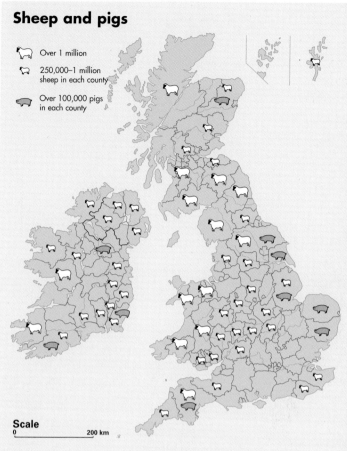

- Over 1 million
- 250,000–1 million sheep in each county
- Over 100,000 pigs in each county

Scale
0 — 200 km

Land use in the UK

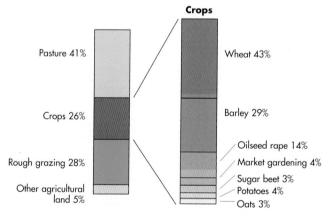

Crops

- Pasture 41%
- Crops 26%
- Rough grazing 28%
- Other agricultural land 5%

- Wheat 43%
- Barley 29%
- Oilseed rape 14%
- Market gardening 4%
- Sugar beet 3%
- Potatoes 4%
- Oats 3%

How much of our food is grown in the UK?

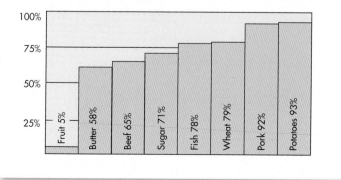

- Fruit 5%
- Butter 58%
- Beef 65%
- Sugar 71%
- Fish 78%
- Wheat 79%
- Pork 92%
- Potatoes 93%

Fishing

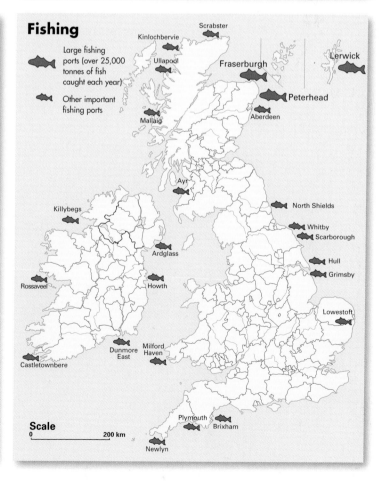

- Large fishing ports (over 25,000 tonnes of fish caught each year)
- Other important fishing ports

Scrabster
Kinlochbervie
Ullapool
Fraserburgh
Lerwick
Peterhead
Aberdeen
Mallaig
Ayr
Killybegs
North Shields
Whitby
Scarborough
Ardglass
Hull
Grimsby
Rossaveel
Howth
Lowestoft
Dunmore East
Milford Haven
Castletownbere
Plymouth
Brixham
Newlyn

Scale
0 — 200 km

Work, industry and energy

Total employment

The number of people working

- Over 4 million
- 3–4 million
- 2–3 million
- Under 2 million

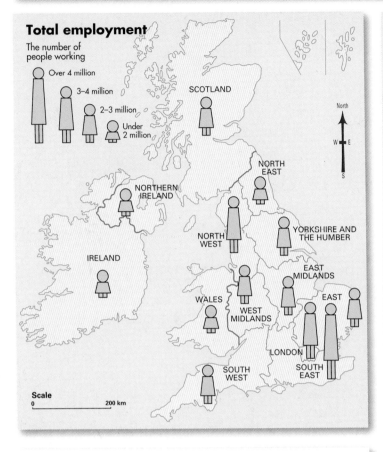

SCOTLAND

NORTHERN IRELAND

NORTH EAST

IRELAND

NORTH WEST

YORKSHIRE AND THE HUMBER

EAST MIDLANDS

WALES

WEST MIDLANDS

EAST

LONDON

SOUTH EAST

SOUTH WEST

Scale
0   200 km

Employment in services

- Over 85%
- 75 – 85%
- Under 75%

Manufacturing industries are industries which make things. Some examples of manufactured goods are cars, steel, textiles and clothes.

Service industries do not make things. They provide a service to people. Shops, hotels and banks are examples of service industries.

Unemployment

% of the workforce who are unemployed

- 8 – 10%
- Over 10%

Employment in manufacturing

% of the workforce who are employed in manufacturing

- 15 – 20%
- Over 20%

Employment in agriculture

% of the workforce who are employed in agriculture, forestry and fishing

- 2 – 10%
- Over 10%

Sources of energy used in the United Kingdom

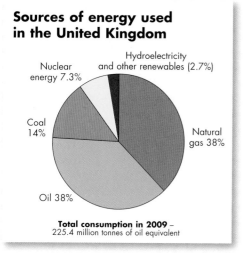

Nuclear energy 7.3%

Hydroelectricity and other renewables (2.7%)

Coal 14%

Oil 38%

Natural gas 38%

Total consumption in 2009 –
225.4 million tonnes of oil equivalent

Electricity generation in the United Kingdom (1980–2009)

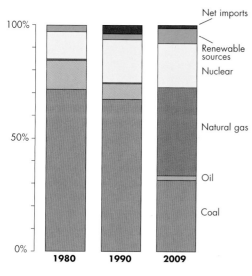

Net imports

Renewable sources

Nuclear

Natural gas

Oil

Coal

100%

50%

0%

1980   1990   2009

This bar-chart shows the different types of fuel that are used to make electricity in the UK. The use of coal and oil in the generation of electricity has dropped between 1980 and 2009. However, the use of natural gas has greatly increased.

Renewable energy

Renewable sources used to generate electricity (in million tonnes of oil equivalent)

	1998	2002	2006	2009
Biofuels	0.9	1.8	3.2	3.6
Hydroelectricity	0.4	0.4	0.4	0.5
Wind Power	0.1	0.1	0.4	0.8
Total renewable energy	1.4	2.3	4.0	4.9

In 2009 6.7% of electricity in the UK was generated by renewable energy sources. This is short of the government's target to increase this to 10% by 2010 and 20% by 2020.

Energy sources in Great Britain and Ireland

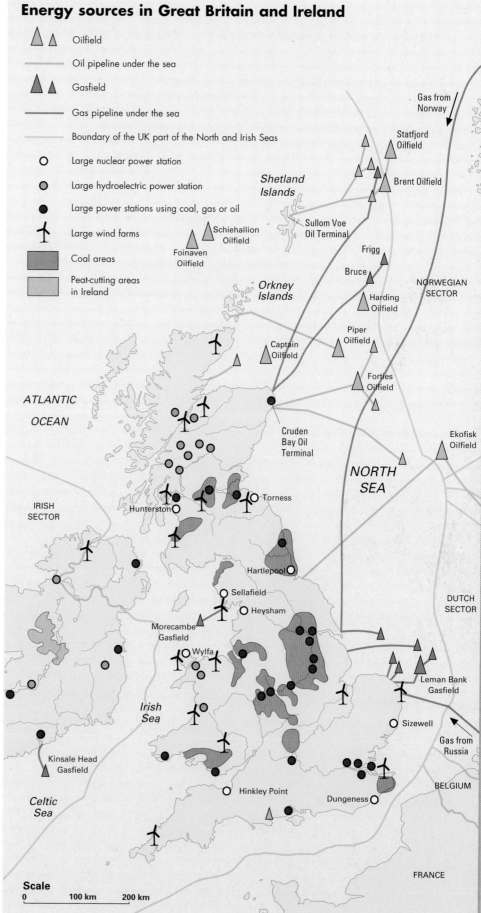

△ △ Oilfield

——— Oil pipeline under the sea

▲ ▲ Gasfield

——— Gas pipeline under the sea

——— Boundary of the UK part of the North and Irish Seas

○ Large nuclear power station

◐ Large hydroelectric power station

● Large power stations using coal, gas or oil

⊤ Large wind farms

▨ Coal areas

▨ Peat-cutting areas in Ireland

Gas from Norway

Statfjord Oilfield

Shetland Islands

Brent Oilfield

Sullom Voe Oil Terminal

Frigg

Bruce

NORWEGIAN SECTOR

Schiehallion Oilfield

Foinaven Oilfield

Harding Oilfield

Orkney Islands

Piper Oilfield

Captain Oilfield

Forties Oilfield

ATLANTIC OCEAN

Cruden Bay Oil Terminal

Ekofisk Oilfield

NORTH SEA

IRISH SECTOR

Torness

Hunterston

Hartlepool

DUTCH SECTOR

Sellafield

Heysham

Morecambe Gasfield

Wylfa

Leman Bank Gasfield

Irish Sea

Sizewell

Kinsale Head Gasfield

Gas from Russia

BELGIUM

Celtic Sea

Hinkley Point

Dungeness

FRANCE

Scale

0   100 km   200 km

15

Transport

There are about 380 thousand kilometres of road in the UK. The total number of cars, buses, lorries and motorbikes is 26 million. That is almost half the number of people in the UK. The maps on this page show the motorways and some main roads in the UK and the number of cars in the different regions. At the bottom of the page there are tables showing the road distances between important towns.

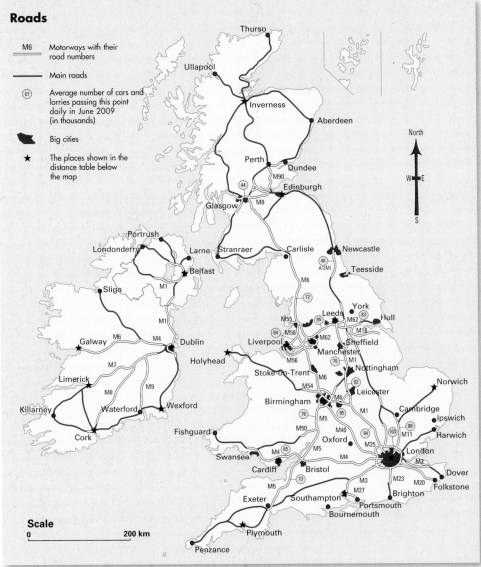

Roads

M6	Motorways with their road numbers
——	Main roads
(67)	Average number of cars and lorries passing this point daily in June 2009 (in thousands)
	Big cities
★	The places shown in the distance table below the map

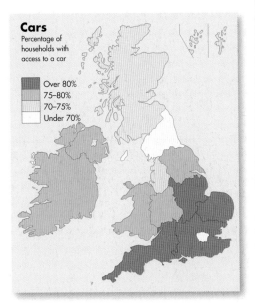

Cars

Percentage of households with access to a car

	Over 80%
	75–80%
	70–75%
	Under 70%

Scale

0 ——————— 200 km

Road distances

The distance tables are in kilometres, but distances on road signposts in the UK are in miles.
A mile is longer than a kilometre.
1 mile = 1.6 kilometres. 1 kilometre = 0.6 mile.

UK	Birmingham	Cardiff	Edinburgh	Holyhead	Inverness	Leeds	Liverpool	London	Manchester	Norwich	Plymouth	Southampton
Birmingham		163	460	246	716	179	151	179	130	249	320	206
Cardiff	163		587	341	843	341	264	249	277	381	259	192
Edinburgh	460	587		489	256	320	338	608	336	586	790	669
Holyhead	246	341	489		745	262	151	420	198	481	528	455
Inverness	716	843	256	745		579	605	864	604	842	1049	925
Leeds	179	341	320	262	579		119	306	64	277	502	378
Liverpool	151	264	338	151	605	119		330	55	360	452	357
London	179	249	608	420	864	306	330		309	172	343	127
Manchester	130	277	336	198	604	64	55	309		306	457	325
Norwich	249	381	586	481	842	277	360	172	306		515	299
Plymouth	320	259	790	528	1049	502	452	343	457	515		246
Southampton	206	192	669	455	925	378	357	127	325	299	246	

Ireland	Belfast	Cork	Dublin	Galway	Limerick	Wexford
Belfast		418	160	300	222	306
Cork	418		257	193	97	190
Dublin	160	257		210	193	137
Galway	300	193	210		97	249
Limerick	222	97	193	97		193
Wexford	306	190	137	249	193	

Railways

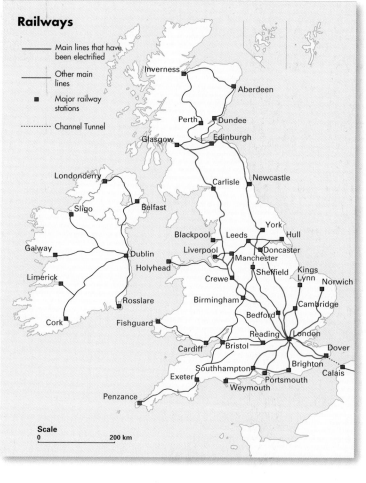

Legend:
- Main lines that have been electrified
- Other main lines
- ■ Major railway stations
- Channel Tunnel

Scale
0 — 200 km

Manchester – the daily flow of people

Cars coming into Manchester

Cars going out of Manchester

Number of cars in thousands

Time: 7am 8 9 10 11 12 1 2 3 4 5 6 7pm

High-speed rail

The map shows high-speed rail lines in Europe. Trains are able to travel at over 200 km/h on these lines.

Journey time to London by train UK cities

- Birmingham — 162 km
- Penzance — 410 km
- Inverness — 723 km

European cities (via Channel Tunnel)

- Paris — 334 km
- Brussels — 321 km

Hours: 0 2 4 6 8 10

Ports and ferries

Legend:
- Major ports
- Other ports
- These ports are handling mainly fuel
- Important canals and rivers carrying goods
- Passenger ferries

Scale
0 — 200 km

Airports

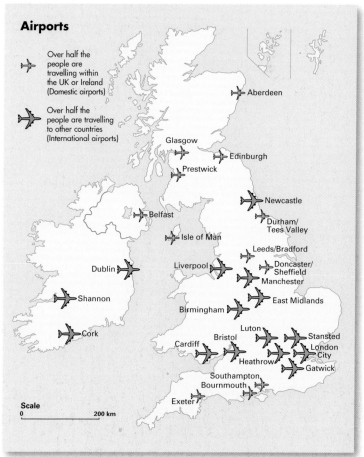

Legend:
- ✈ Over half the people are travelling within the UK or Ireland (Domestic airports)
- ✈ Over half the people are travelling to other countries (International airports)

Scale
0 — 200 km

17

Conservation and tourism

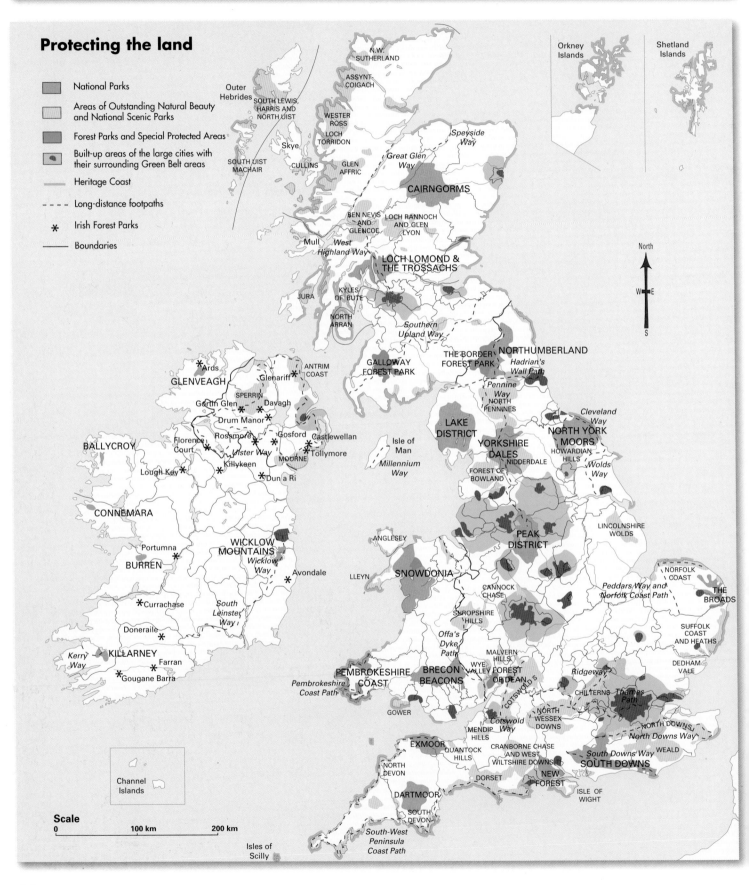

Protecting the land

Legend:
- National Parks
- Areas of Outstanding Natural Beauty and National Scenic Parks
- Forest Parks and Special Protected Areas
- Built-up areas of the large cities with their surrounding Green Belt areas
- Heritage Coast
- Long-distance footpaths
- ✳ Irish Forest Parks
- Boundaries

North
W E S

Orkney Islands

Shetland Islands

N.W. SUTHERLAND
ASSYNT-COIGACH
Outer Hebrides
SOUTH LEWIS, HARRIS AND NORTH UIST
WESTER ROSS
LOCH TORRIDON
Skye
SOUTH UIST MACHAIR
CULLINS
GLEN AFFRIC
Speyside Way
Great Glen Way
CAIRNGORMS
BEN NEVIS AND GLENCOE
LOCH RANNOCH AND GLEN LYON
Mull
West Highland Way
LOCH LOMOND & THE TROSSACHS
JURA
KYLES OF BUTE
NORTH ARRAN
Southern Upland Way
GALLOWAY FOREST PARK
THE BORDER FOREST PARK
NORTHUMBERLAND
Hadrian's Wall Path
Pennine Way
NORTH PENNINES
Cleveland Way
LAKE DISTRICT
YORKSHIRE DALES
NORTH YORK MOORS
HOWARDIAN HILLS
NIDDERDALE
Wolds Way
FOREST OF BOWLAND
Isle of Man
Millennium Way
PEAK DISTRICT
LINCOLNSHIRE WOLDS
ANGLESEY
LLEYN
SNOWDONIA
CANNOCK CHASE
SHROPSHIRE HILLS
Offa's Dyke Path
MALVERN HILLS
WYE VALLEY
FOREST OF DEAN
Peddars Way and Norfolk Coast Path
NORFOLK COAST
THE BROADS
SUFFOLK COAST AND HEATHS
DEDHAM VALE
Ridgeway
CHILTERNS
Thames Path
PEMBROKESHIRE COAST
BRECON BEACONS
Pembrokeshire Coast Path
GOWER
COTSWOLDS
Cotswold Way
MENDIP HILLS
NORTH WESSEX DOWNS
CRANBORNE CHASE AND WEST WILTSHIRE DOWNS
NORTH DOWNS
North Downs Way
WEALD
SOUTH DOWNS
South Downs Way
EXMOOR
QUANTOCK HILLS
DORSET
NEW FOREST
ISLE OF WIGHT
NORTH DEVON
DARTMOOR
SOUTH DEVON
South-West Peninsula Coast Path
Isles of Scilly

Ireland
✳ Ards
GLENVEAGH
✳ Glenariff
ANTRIM COAST
SPERRIN
✳ Gortin Glen
✳ Davagh
✳ Drum Manor
BALLYCROY
✳ Florence Court
✳ Rossmore
✳ Gosford
✳ Castlewellan
Ulster Way
MOURNE
✳ Tollymore
✳ Lough Key
✳ Killykeen
✳ Dun a Ri
CONNEMARA
✳ Portumna
WICKLOW MOUNTAINS
Wicklow Way
BURREN
✳ Avondale
✳ Currachase
South Leinster Way
Doneraile
✳
Kerry Way
KILLARNEY
✳ Farran
✳ Gougane Barra

Channel Islands

Scale
0   100 km   200 km

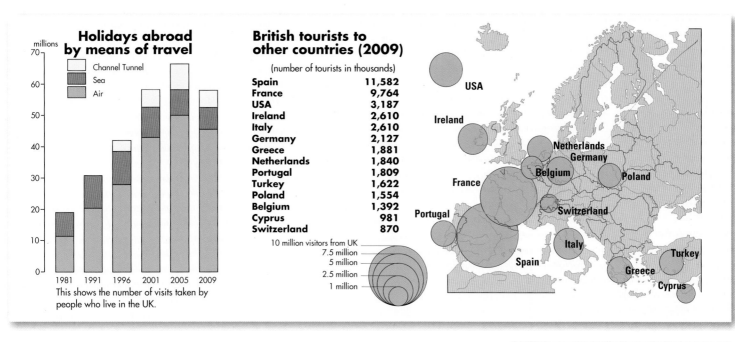

Holidays abroad by means of travel

millions

Channel Tunnel
Sea
Air

1981 1991 1996 2001 2005 2009

This shows the number of visits taken by people who live in the UK.

British tourists to other countries (2009)

(number of tourists in thousands)

Spain	11,582
France	9,764
USA	3,187
Ireland	2,610
Italy	2,610
Germany	2,127
Greece	1,881
Netherlands	1,840
Portugal	1,809
Turkey	1,622
Poland	1,554
Belgium	1,392
Cyprus	981
Switzerland	870

10 million visitors from UK
7.5 million
5 million
2.5 million
1 million

Tourism

● Main holiday cities and towns

● Major tourist attractions

Scale
0   200 km

Visitors to the UK from other countries (2009)

(number of visitors in thousands)

France	3,784
Ireland	2,948
USA	2,887
Germany	2,780
Spain	2,164
Netherlands	1,715
Italy	1,221
Poland	1,041
Australia	912
Belgium	903
Switzerland	701
Canada	687
Sweden	604

Tourist attractions (2009)

(number of visitors in millions)

British Museum, London	5.6
National Gallery, London	4.8
Tate Modern, London	4.7
Natural History Museum, London	4.1
Science Museum, London	2.8
Tower of London	2.4
Victoria and Albert Museum, London	2.3
Natural Portrait Gallery, London	2.0
St Paul's Cathedral, London	1.8
River Lee Country Park, Hertfordshire	1.5
Tate Britain, London	1.5
Flamingo Land, Kirby Misperton	1.4
British Library, London	1.4
Westminster Abbey, London	1.4
Lake Windermere	1.3
Kew Gardens, London	1.3
Fairlands Valley Park, Hertfordshire	1.3
Chester Zoo	1.2
Thetford Forest Park	1.2
Eden Project, Cornwall	1.1
London Zoo	1.1

Water

Rainfall areas – wet and dry

The wet west
Monthly rainfall graph for Grasmere

Year – 1,851 mm

mm
200
150
100
50
0
J F M A M J J A S O N D

The dry east
Monthly rainfall graph for Cambridge

Year – 558 mm

mm
200
150
100
50
0
J F M A M J J A S O N D

In these areas a lot of rain (over 1,000 mm) falls nearly every year

In these areas less than 1,000 mm of rain falls

Scale
0   200 km

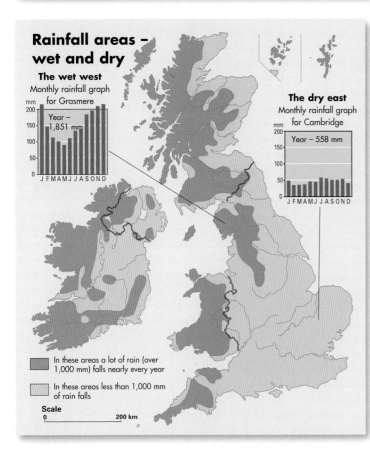

Reservoirs and boreholes

Big reservoirs

Areas where water is got out of the ground with boreholes

The water flows to where it is used, either along rivers or through pipelines

The big cities where a lot of water is needed

North

Loch Lomond
Loch Katrine
Kielder Res.
Thirlmere
Cow Green Res.
Haweswater
Poulaphouca Res.
Rutland Water
Elan Valley
Grafham Water

Scale
0   200 km

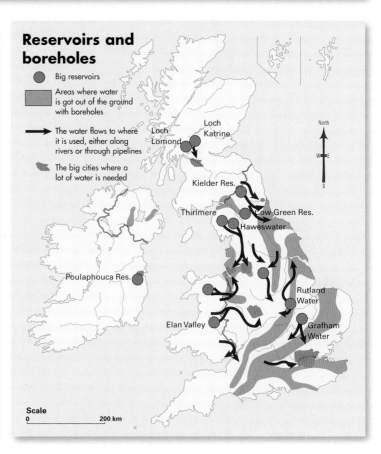

Sources of river pollution

Pollution from factories goes into the air.

Acid rain from pollution by industry and vehicle exhausts.

Industry
Chemicals and wastes go into the river.

Homes
Chemical and sewage wastes.

Waste from industry and rubbish from houses is buried.

River pollution flows to lakes and the sea.

Agriculture
Pesticides, sewage waste and soil carried away by water.

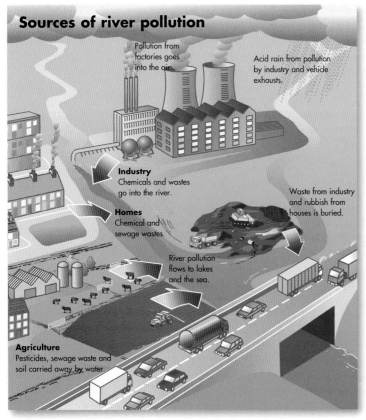

River pollution

Badly polluted rivers

Over 15%

10% – 15%

5% – 10%

Under 5%
of the rivers in these areas are of poor or bad quality

No information for Ireland

Sea areas where sewage and other waste is dumped

Scale
0   200 km

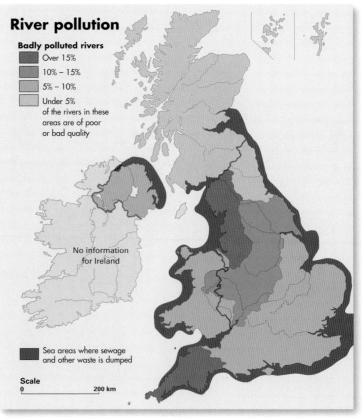

The average UK household uses 355 litres of water a day. Up to 135,000 million litres of water are used each day in the UK. Over half the water is used by people in their homes. About a third is used to make electricity. The rest is used in farms and factories. On the right are some of the ways that water is used in the home:

To make one car can use up to 30,000 litres of water. To brew one pint of beer needs 8 pints of water.

Domestic appliances – water usage

	(per wash)
Washing machine	80 litres
Bath	80 litres
Dishwasher	35 litres
Shower	35 litres
Toilet flush	6 litres

Flooding

Around 5 million people, in 2 million properties, live in flood risk areas in England and Wales. In summer 2007 there were several periods of extreme rainfall which led to widespread flooding.

The Environment Agency has an important role in warning people about the risk of flooding, and in reducing the likelihood of flooding from rivers and the sea.

Flood risk in England and Wales

■ Areas at greatest risk from flooding

◊ Counties worst affected by flooding in summer 2007

The water cycle

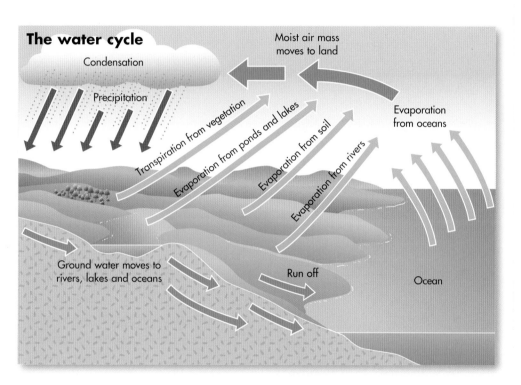

Domestic water and sewage (the man-made water cycle)

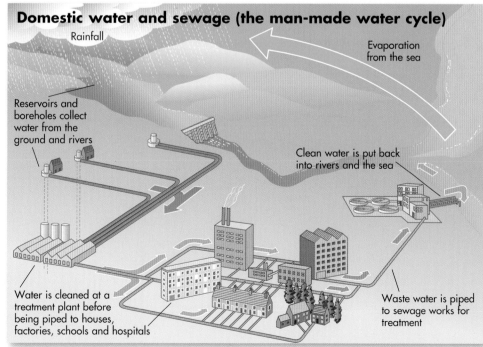

21

Counties and regions

Names

The map on the left shows the **British Isles**, which is made up of the two large islands of **Great Britain** and **Ireland** and many smaller islands. There are two countries, the **United Kingdom** and **Ireland**. The full name of the United Kingdom is The United Kingdom of Great Britain and Northern Ireland. It has four parts: **England**, **Wales**, **Scotland** and **Northern Ireland**. It is known for short as the United Kingdom, UK or Britain. The whole country is often wrongly called England. The Republic of Ireland is sometimes shown as Eire (on its stamps), which is the name of Ireland in the Irish language.

■ ● Capital cities

These are the names for some of the different areas in the British Isles

Counties and regions

The map shows the Standard Regions of the United Kingdom. The boundaries follow those of the counties shown on page 23. Large bodies like the Health Service, Water or Electricity divide the country up into their own regions. Ireland is divided into four historic provinces.

Scale
0   200 km

Counties and unitary authorities

England and Wales are divided into counties, unitary authorities and boroughs. The counties are divided into districts, and the districts into parishes and wards. Scotland is divided into regions and unitary authorities, and Northern Ireland into districts.

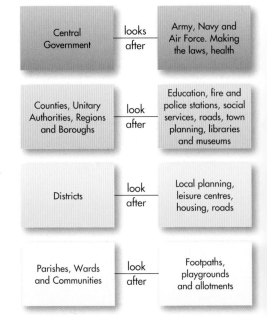

Central Government	looks after	Army, Navy and Air Force. Making the laws, health
Counties, Unitary Authorities, Regions and Boroughs	look after	Education, fire and police stations, social services, roads, town planning, libraries and museums
Districts	look after	Local planning, leisure centres, housing, roads
Parishes, Wards and Communities	look after	Footpaths, playgrounds and allotments

Area data

	Area in square kilometres
England	130,439
Wales	20,768
Scotland	77,167
Northern Ireland	13,483
United Kingdom	**241,857**
Isle of Man	**572**
Channel Islands	**195**
Ireland	**68,896**

The Channel Islands and the Isle of Man are dependencies of the Crown and have their own parliaments. They are not part of the United Kingdom.

The six counties are shown in Northern Ireland. It is divided for local government into 26 districts.

The map shows the 6 counties in Northern Ireland, the 32 unitary authorities in Scotland, the 22 unitary authorities in Wales, and the 56 unitary authorities and 27 counties in England. Authorities which are too small to name on the map are numbered and listed separately.

SCOTLAND
1. ABERDEEN CITY
2. DUNDEE CITY
3. WEST DUNBARTONSHIRE
4. EAST DUNBARTONSHIRE
5. CITY OF GLASGOW
6. INVERCLYDE
7. RENFREWSHIRE
8. EAST RENFREWSHIRE
9. NORTH LANARKSHIRE
10. FALKIRK
11. CLACKMANNANSHIRE
12. WEST LOTHIAN
13. CITY OF EDINBURGH
14. MIDLOTHIAN

WALES
15. SWANSEA
16. NEATH PORT TALBOT
17. BRIDGEND
18. RHONDDA CYNON TAFF
19. MERTHYR TYDFIL
20. CAERPHILLY
21. BLAENAU GWENT
22. TORFAEN
23. CARDIFF
24. NEWPORT

ENGLAND
25. HARTLEPOOL
26. DARLINGTON
27. STOCKTON-ON-TEES
28. MIDDLESBROUGH
29. REDCAR AND CLEVELAND
30. BLACKPOOL
31. BLACKBURN WITH DARWEN
32. HALTON
33. WARRINGTON
34. KINGSTON UPON HULL
35. NORTH EAST LINCOLNSHIRE
36. STOKE-ON-TRENT
37. TELFORD AND WREKIN
38. DERBY CITY
39. CITY OF NOTTINGHAM
40. LEICESTER CITY
41. RUTLAND
42. PETERBOROUGH
43. MILTON KEYNES
44. LUTON
45. NORTH SOMERSET
46. CITY OF BRISTOL
47. BATH AND N. E. SOMERSET
48. SWINDON
49. READING
50. WOKINGHAM
51. WINDSOR AND MAIDENHEAD
52. SLOUGH
53. BRACKNELL FOREST
54. THURROCK
55. SOUTHEND-ON-SEA
56. MEDWAY
57. PLYMOUTH
58. TORBAY
59. POOLE
60. BOURNEMOUTH
61. SOUTHAMPTON
62. PORTSMOUTH
63. BRIGHTON AND HOVE
64. CHESHIRE WEST AND CHESTER
65. CHESHIRE EAST
66. BEDFORD
67. CENTRAL BEDFORDSHIRE

Scale

0   100 km   200 km

● Capital cities

23

England and Wales

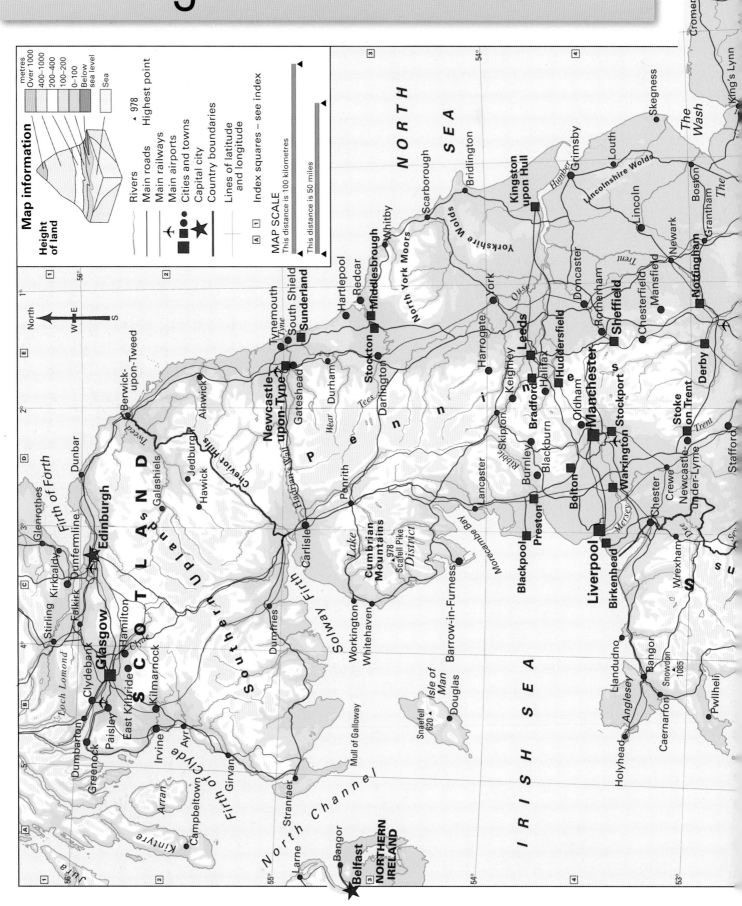

Map information

Height of land

metres	
	Over 1000
	400–1000
	200–400
	100–200
	0–100
	Below sea level
	Sea

▲ 978 Highest point

Rivers
Main roads
Main railways
✈ Main airports
● Cities and towns
★ Capital city
Country boundaries
Lines of latitude and longitude

A · 1 Index squares – see index

MAP SCALE
This distance is 100 kilometres
This distance is 50 miles

24

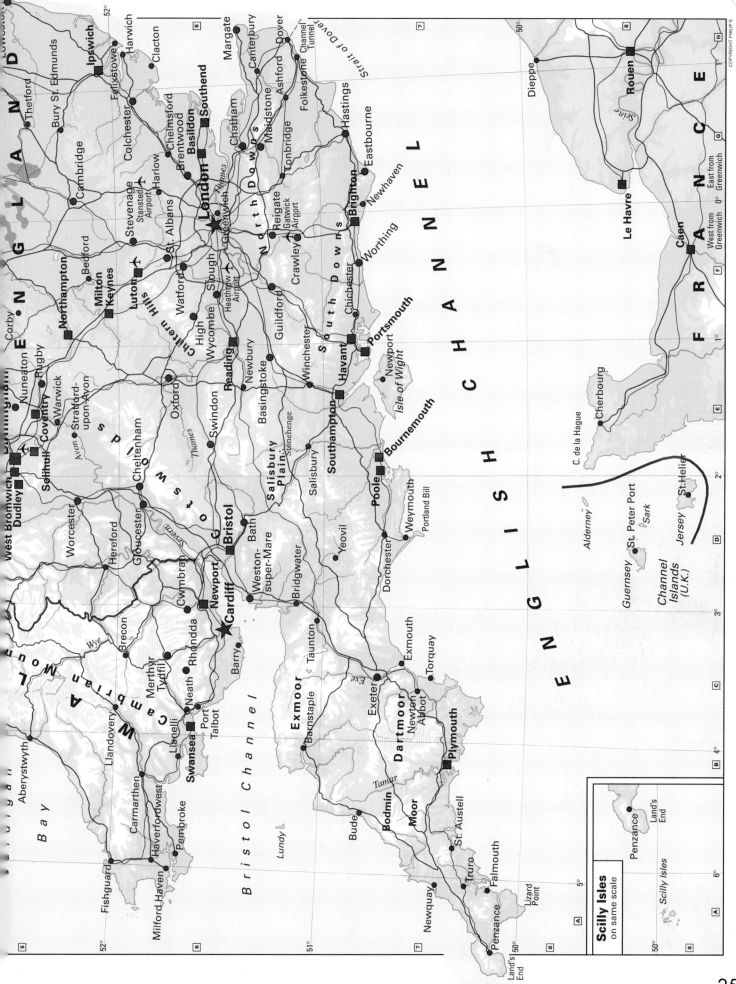

Scotland and Ireland

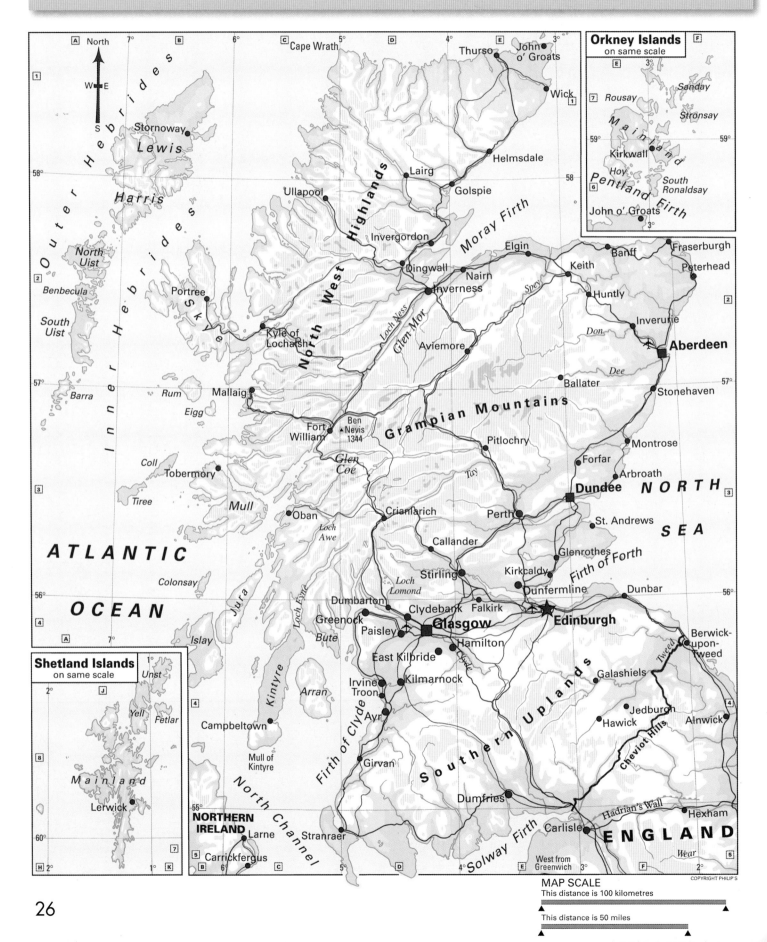

Orkney Islands
on same scale

Sanday
Rousay
Stronsay
Mainland
Kirkwall
Hoy
South Ronaldsay
Pentland Firth
John o' Groats

Shetland Islands
on same scale

Unst
Yell
Fetlar
Mainland
Lerwick

Cape Wrath
Thurso
John o' Groats
Wick
Stornoway
Lewis
Harris
Ullapool
Lairg
Helmsdale
Golspie
Invergordon
Elgin
Banff
Fraserburgh
Keith
Peterhead
Outer Hebrides
North Uist
Benbecula
South Uist
Dingwall
Nairn
Inverness
Huntly
Portree
Skye
Inverurie
North West Highlands
Loch Ness
Glen Mor
Spey
Don
Aberdeen
Kyle of Lochalsh
Aviemore
Dee
Barra
Rum
Eigg
Mallaig
Ballater
Stonehaven
Fort William
Ben Nevis 1344
Grampian Mountains
Montrose
Coll
Tobermory
Glen Coe
Pitlochry
Forfar
Arbroath
Tiree
Mull
Tay
Dundee
NORTH
Oban
Loch Awe
Crianlarich
Perth
St. Andrews
SEA
Callander
Glenrothes
Firth of Forth
ATLANTIC
Colonsay
Stirling
Kirkcaldy
Loch Lomond
Dunfermline
Dunbar
OCEAN
Jura
Dumbarton
Clydebank
Falkirk
Edinburgh
Greenock
Glasgow
Paisley
Hamilton
Berwick-upon-Tweed
Islay
Bute
East Kilbride
Tweed
Kintyre
Arran
Irvine
Troon
Kilmarnock
Clyde
Galashiels
Jedburgh
Campbeltown
Ayr
Hawick
Alnwick
Southern Uplands
Mull of Kintyre
Girvan
Cheviot Hills
NORTHERN IRELAND
Larne
Stranraer
Dumfries
Hadrian's Wall
Hexham
North Channel
Carrickfergus
Firth of Clyde
Solway Firth
Carlisle
ENGLAND
West from Greenwich
Wear

MAP SCALE
This distance is 100 kilometres

This distance is 50 miles

COPYRIGHT PHILIP'S

26

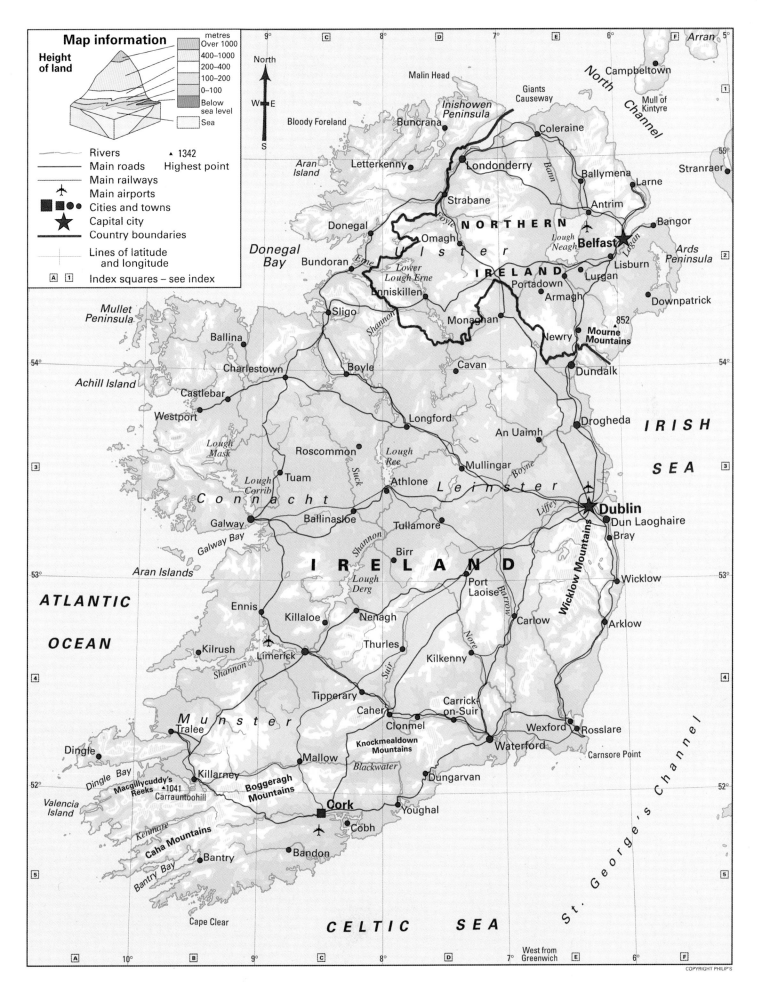

Map information

Height of land

metres
Over 1000
400–1000
200–400
100–200
0–100
Below sea level
Sea

Rivers
Main roads
Main railways
Main airports
Cities and towns
Capital city
Country boundaries
Lines of latitude and longitude
Index squares – see index

▲ 1342 Highest point

North
W—E
S

Arran

Campbeltown
Mull of Kintyre
North Channel
Malin Head
Giants Causeway
Inishowen Peninsula
Bloody Foreland
Buncrana
Coleraine
Stranraer
Aran Island
Letterkenny
Londonderry
Ballymena
Larne
Strabane
Antrim
Bangor
Donegal
Omagh
NORTHERN
Lough Neagh
Belfast
Ards Peninsula
Donegal Bay
Bundoran
Erne
Lower Lough Erne
IRELAND
Lisburn
Lurgan
Enniskillen
Portadown
Armagh
Downpatrick
Mullet Peninsula
Sligo
Shannon
Monaghan
Newry
852
Mourne Mountains
Ballina
Boyle
Cavan
Dundalk
Charlestown
54°
54°
Achill Island
Castlebar
Longford
Drogheda
IRISH
Westport
An Uaimh
SEA
Lough Mask
Roscommon
Lough Ree
Mullingar
Boyne
Tuam
Lough Corrib
Slck
Athlone
Leinster
Galway
Ballinasloe
Liffey
Dublin
Galway Bay
Dun Laoghaire
Connacht
Shannon
Birr
Bray
Aran Islands
53°
Lough Derg
IRELAND
Wicklow Mountains
53°
ATLANTIC
Ennis
Port Laoise
Wicklow
OCEAN
Killaloe
Nenagh
Carlow
Arklow
Kilrush
Thurles
Barrow
Nore
Limerick
Kilkenny
Shannon
Tipperary
Suir
Carrick-on-Suir
Wexford
Caher
Rosslare
Dingle
Munster
Clonmel
Carnsore Point
Tralee
Mallow
Knockmealdown Mountains
Waterford
Dingle Bay
Killarney
Blackwater
Dungarvan
52°
Macgillycuddy's Reeks ▲1041
Boggeragh Mountains
52°
Valencia Island
Carrauntoohill
Cork
Kenmare
Caha Mountains
Youghal
Cobh
St. George's Channel
Bantry
Bandon
Bantry Bay
Cape Clear
CELTIC SEA
West from Greenwich

COPYRIGHT PHILIP'S

The Earth as a planet

Relative sizes of the planets

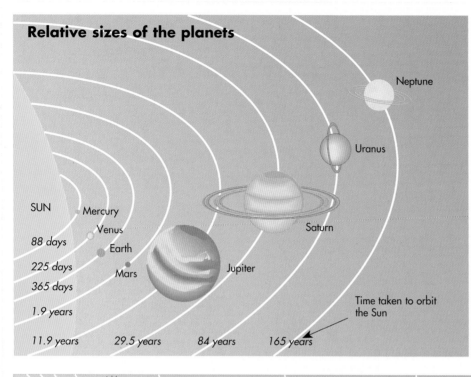

SUN

Mercury
88 days

Venus
225 days

Earth
365 days

Mars
1.9 years

11.9 years

29.5 years

84 years

165 years

Jupiter

Saturn

Uranus

Neptune

Time taken to orbit the Sun

The Solar System

The Earth is one of the eight planets that orbit the Sun. These two diagrams show how big the planets are, how far they are away from the Sun and how long they take to orbit the Sun. The diagram on the left shows how the planets closest to the Sun have the shortest orbits. The Earth takes 365 days (a year) to go round the Sun. The Earth is the fifth largest planet. It is much smaller than Jupiter and Saturn which are the largest planets.

Distances of the planets from the Sun in millions of kilometres

Mercury 58

Venus 108

Earth 150

Mars 228

Asteroids

Jupiter 778

Saturn 1,430

Uranus 2,870

Neptune 4,500

Planet Earth

The Earth spins as if it is on a rod – its axis. The axis would come out of the Earth at two points. The northern point is called the North Pole and the southern point is called the South Pole. The distance between the Poles through the centre of the Earth is 12,700 km.

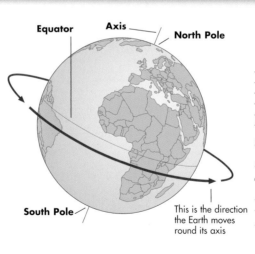

Equator

Axis

North Pole

South Pole

This is the direction the Earth moves round its axis

It takes a day (24 hours) for the Earth to rotate on its axis. It is light (day) when it faces the Sun and dark (night) when it faces away. See the diagram below. The Equator is a line round the Earth which is halfway between the Poles. It is 40,000 km long.

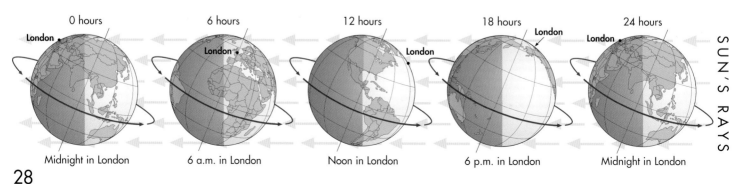

0 hours
London
Midnight in London

6 hours
London
6 a.m. in London

12 hours
London
Noon in London

18 hours
London
6 p.m. in London

24 hours
London
Midnight in London

SUN'S RAYS

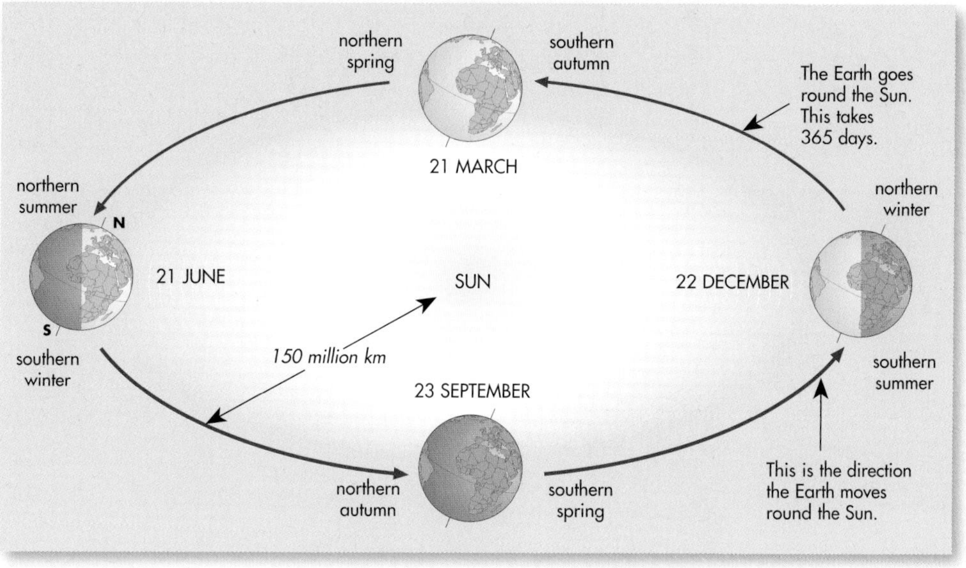

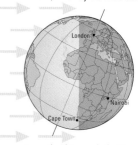

The year and seasons

The Earth is always tilted at 66½°. It moves around the Sun. This movement gives us the seasons of the year. In June the northern hemisphere tilts towards the Sun so it is summer. Six months later, in December, the Earth has rotated halfway round the Sun. It is then summer in the southern hemisphere.

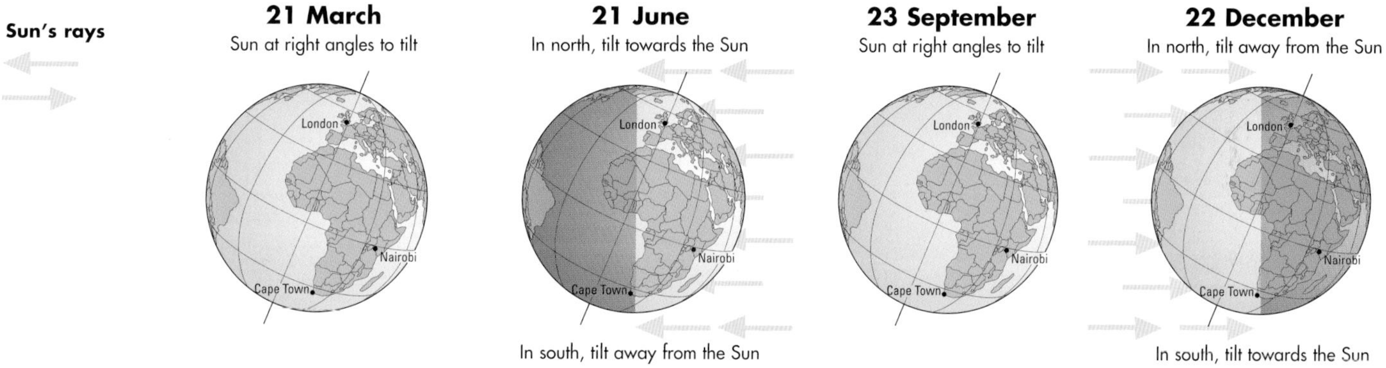

(Top diagram labels)

The Earth goes round the Sun. This takes 365 days.

- northern spring / southern autumn — 21 MARCH
- northern summer / southern winter — 21 JUNE
- northern winter / southern summer — 22 DECEMBER
- northern autumn / southern spring — 23 SEPTEMBER
- SUN
- 150 million km
- This is the direction the Earth moves round the Sun.

Sun's rays

21 March	21 June	23 September	22 December
Sun at right angles to tilt	In north, tilt towards the Sun	Sun at right angles to tilt	In north, tilt away from the Sun

(Globe labels: London, Nairobi, Cape Town)

In south, tilt away from the Sun — (21 June)
In south, tilt towards the Sun — (22 December)

Season	Northern Spring Southern Autumn			Northern Summer Southern Winter			Northern Autumn Southern Spring			Northern Winter Southern Summer		
City	London	Nairobi	Cape Town	London	Nairobi	Cape Town	London	Nairobi	Cape Town	London	Nairobi	Cape Town
Latitude	51°N	1°S	34°S	51°N	1°S	34°S	51°N	1°S	34°S	51°N	1°S	34°S
Day length	12 hrs	12 hrs	12 hrs	16 hrs	12 hrs	10 hrs	12 hrs	12 hrs	12 hrs	8 hrs	12 hrs	14 hrs
Night length	12 hrs	12 hrs	12 hrs	8 hrs	12 hrs	14 hrs	12 hrs	12 hrs	12 hrs	16 hrs	12 hrs	10 hrs
Temperature	7°C	21°C	21°C	16°C	18°C	13°C	15°C	19°C	14°C	5°C	19°C	20°C

The Moon

The Moon is about a quarter the size of the Earth. It orbits the Earth in just over 27 days (almost a month). The Moon is round but we on Earth see only the parts lit by the Sun. This makes it look as if the Moon is a different shape at different times of the month. These are known as the phases of the Moon and they are shown in this diagram.

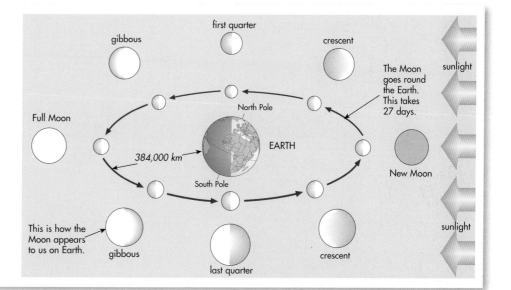

(Moon diagram labels) first quarter, gibbous, crescent, sunlight, The Moon goes round the Earth. This takes 27 days. North Pole, EARTH, 384,000 km, South Pole, New Moon, Full Moon, This is how the Moon appears to us on Earth. gibbous, last quarter, crescent, sunlight

Mountains and rivers

The surface of the Earth is continually being shaped by movements of the Earth's crust. Volcanoes are formed and earthquakes are caused in this way. Rivers also shape the landscape as they flow on their way to the sea.

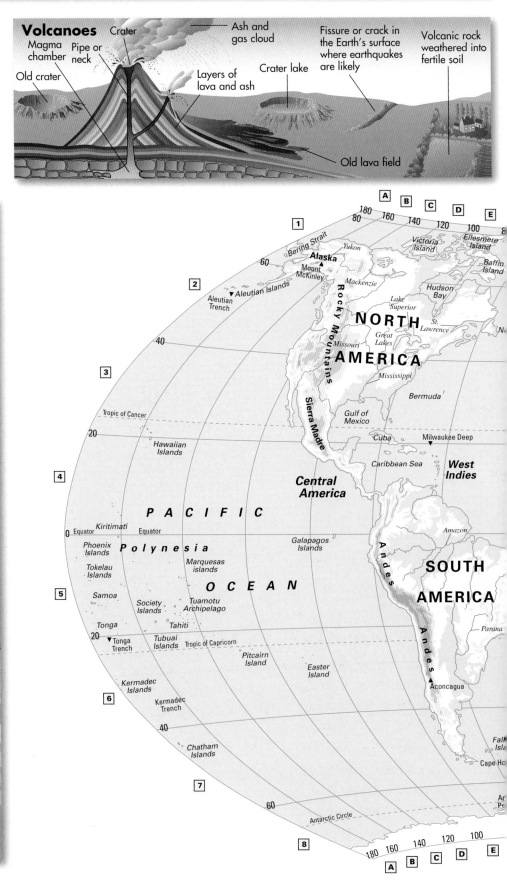

Volcanoes
Crater
Ash and gas cloud
Magma chamber
Pipe or neck
Old crater
Layers of lava and ash
Crater lake
Fissure or crack in the Earth's surface where earthquakes are likely
Volcanic rock weathered into fertile soil
Old lava field

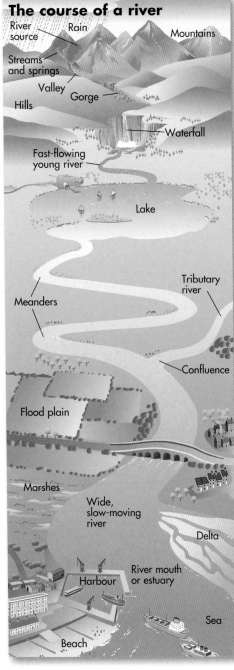

The course of a river

River source
Rain
Mountains
Streams and springs
Valley
Gorge
Hills
Waterfall
Fast-flowing young river
Lake
Tributary river
Meanders
Confluence
Flood plain
Marshes
Wide, slow-moving river
Delta
Harbour
River mouth or estuary
Sea
Beach

Map labels:

Bering Strait
Yukon
Victoria Island
Ellesmere Island
Alaska
Mount McKinley
Mackenzie
Baffin Island
Aleutian Islands
Aleutian Trench
Lake Superior
Hudson Bay
NORTH AMERICA
Rocky Mountains
St. Lawrence
Great Lakes
Missouri
Mississippi
Bermuda
Tropic of Cancer
Sierra Madre
Gulf of Mexico
Cuba
Milwaukee Deep
Hawaiian Islands
Caribbean Sea
West Indies
Central America
PACIFIC
Equator
Kiritimati
Equator
Galapagos Islands
Amazon
Phoenix Islands
Polynesia
Marquesas islands
Tokelau Islands
SOUTH AMERICA
Andes
OCEAN
Samoa
Society Islands
Tuamotu Archipelago
Tonga
Tahiti
Tonga Trench
Tubuai Islands
Tropic of Capricorn
Parana
Pitcairn Island
Easter Island
Kermadec Islands
Aconcagua
Kermadec Trench
Chatham Islands
Falkland Islands
Cape Horn
Antarctic Circle

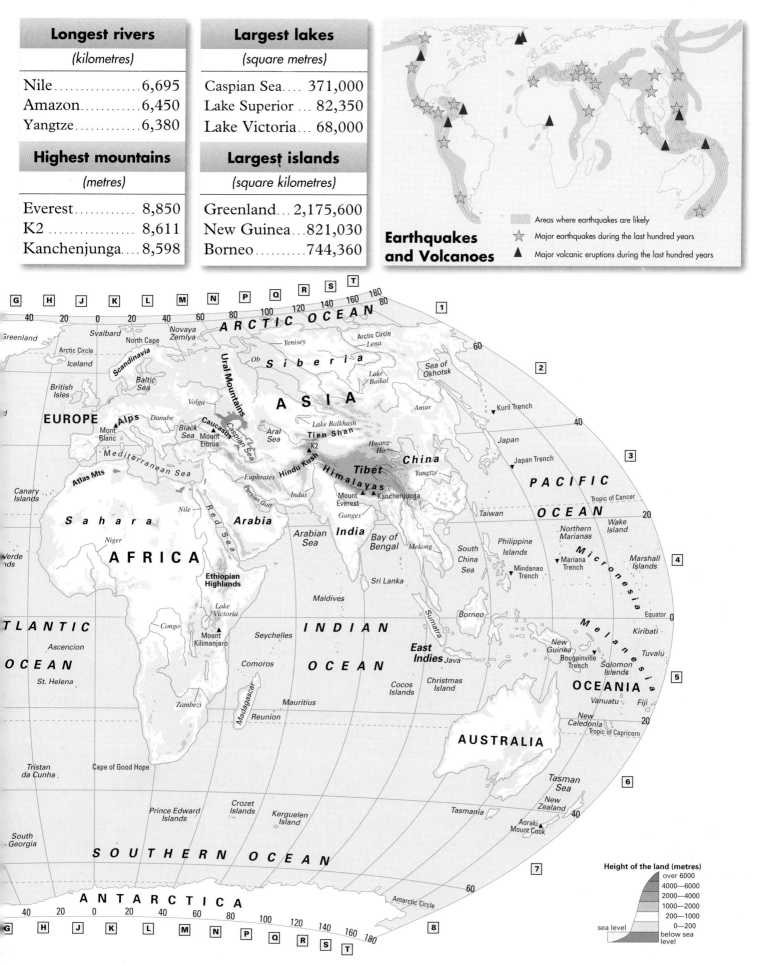

Longest rivers
(kilometres)

Nile	6,695
Amazon	6,450
Yangtze	6,380

Largest lakes
(square metres)

Caspian Sea	371,000
Lake Superior	82,350
Lake Victoria	68,000

Highest mountains
(metres)

Everest	8,850
K2	8,611
Kanchenjunga	8,598

Largest islands
(square kilometres)

Greenland	2,175,600
New Guinea	821,030
Borneo	744,360

Earthquakes and Volcanoes

Areas where earthquakes are likely

★ Major earthquakes during the last hundred years

▲ Major volcanic eruptions during the last hundred years

Height of the land (metres)

over 6000
4000—6000
2000—4000
1000—2000
200—1000
0—200
sea level
below sea level

Climates of the World

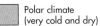

| | Tropical climate (hot and wet) | | Dry climate (desert and steppe) | | Mild climate (warm and wet) | | Continental climate (cold and wet) | | Polar climate (very cold and dry) | | Mountainous areas (where altitude affects climate type) |

Tropical climate (hot and wet)
Heavy rainfall and high temperatures all the year with little difference between the hot and cold months.

Dry climate (desert and steppe)
Many months, often years, without rain. High temperatures in the summer but cooler in winter.

Mild climate (warm and wet)
Rain every month. Warm summers and cool winters.

Continental climate (cold and wet)
Mild summers and very cold winters.

Polar climate (very cold and dry)
Very cold at all times, especially in the winter months. Very little rainfall.

Mountainous areas (where altitude affects climate type)
Lower temperatures because the land is high. Heavy rain and snow.

Key to the climate graphs

Total annual rainfall

Average monthly rainfall

Months of the year from January to December

Average monthly temperature in degrees C. When the temperature is below freezing the lines extend below the bottom of the graph.

LONDON 593 mm

MEXICO CITY 709 mm

BAHRAIN 70 mm

MOSCOW 575 mm −10°C

CHURCHILL 410 mm −28°C

EISMITTE 5 mm −45°C

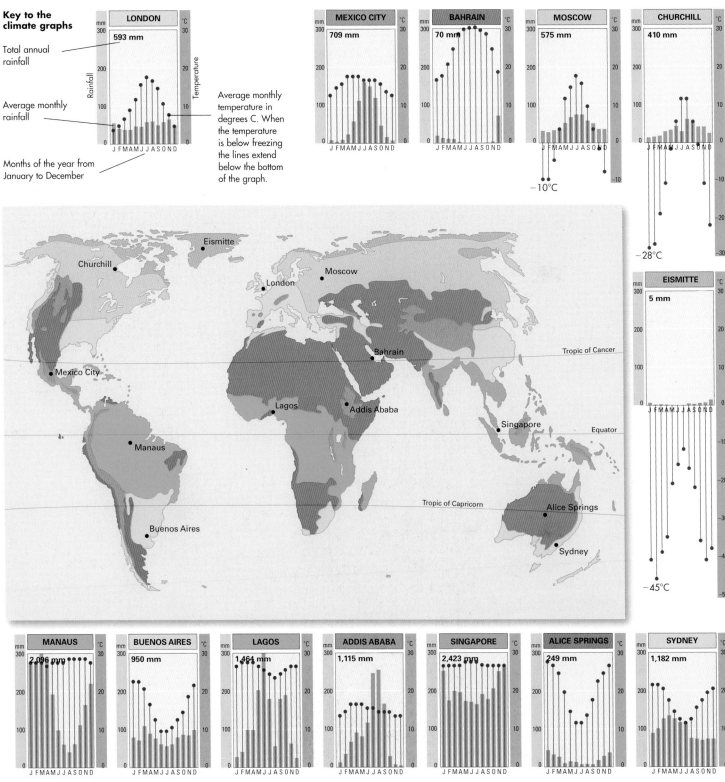

MANAUS 2,096 mm

BUENOS AIRES 950 mm

LAGOS 1,464 mm

ADDIS ABABA 1,115 mm

SINGAPORE 2,423 mm

ALICE SPRINGS 249 mm

SYDNEY 1,182 mm

Annual rainfall

Human, plant and animal life cannot live without water. The map on the right shows how much rain falls in different parts of the world. You can see that there is a lot of rain in some places near the Equator. In other places, like the desert areas of the world, there is very little rain. Few plants or animals can survive there. There is also very little rain in the cold lands of the north.

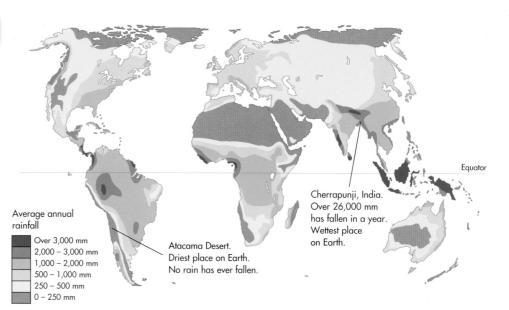

Average annual rainfall

- Over 3,000 mm
- 2,000 – 3,000 mm
- 1,000 – 2,000 mm
- 500 – 1,000 mm
- 250 – 500 mm
- 0 – 250 mm

Cherrapunji, India. Over 26,000 mm has fallen in a year. Wettest place on Earth.

Atacama Desert. Driest place on Earth. No rain has ever fallen.

Equator

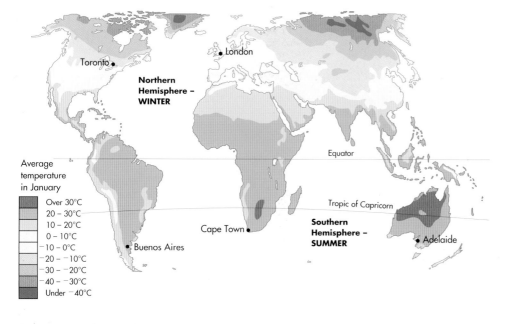

Average temperature in January

- Over 30°C
- 20 – 30°C
- 10 – 20°C
- 0 – 10°C
- –10 – 0°C
- –20 – –10°C
- –30 – –20°C
- –40 – –30°C
- Under –40°C

Toronto
London
Northern Hemisphere – WINTER
Equator
Tropic of Capricorn
Cape Town
Southern Hemisphere – SUMMER
Buenos Aires
Adelaide

January temperature

In December, it is winter in the northern hemisphere. It is hot in the southern continents and cold in the northern continents. The North Pole is tilted away from the sun. It is overhead in the regions around the Tropic of Capricorn. This means that there are about 14 hours of daylight in Buenos Aires, Cape Town and Adelaide, and only about 8 hours in London and Toronto.

June temperature

In June, it is summer in the northern hemisphere and winter in the southern hemisphere. It is warmer in the northern lands and colder in the south. The North Pole is tilted towards the sun. This means that in London and Toronto there are about 16 hours of daylight, but in Buenos Aires, Cape Town and Adelaide there are just under 10 hours.

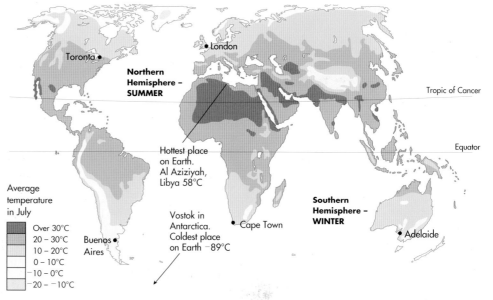

Average temperature in July

- Over 30°C
- 20 – 30°C
- 10 – 20°C
- 0 – 10°C
- –10 – 0°C
- –20 – –10°C

Toronto
London
Northern Hemisphere – SUMMER
Tropic of Cancer
Equator
Hottest place on Earth. Al Aziziyah, Libya 58°C
Vostok in Antarctica. Coldest place on Earth –89°C
Buenos Aires
Cape Town
Southern Hemisphere – WINTER
Adelaide

33

Forests, grasslands and wastes

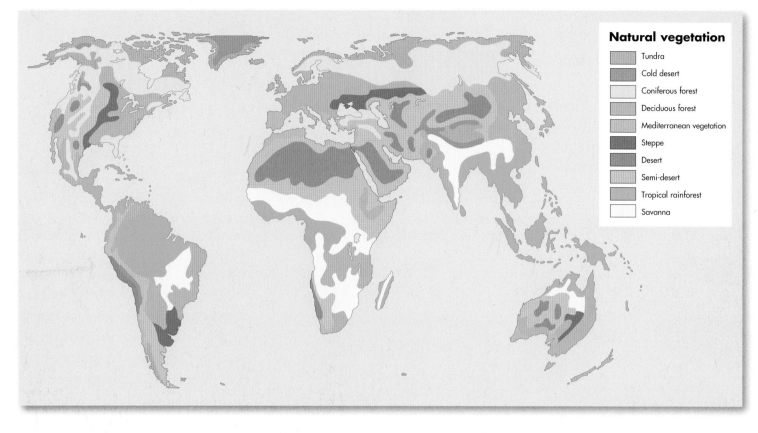

Natural vegetation
- Tundra
- Cold desert
- Coniferous forest
- Deciduous forest
- Mediterranean vegetation
- Steppe
- Desert
- Semi-desert
- Tropical rainforest
- Savanna

The map above shows types of vegetation around the world. The diagram below shows the types of plants which grow on mountains.

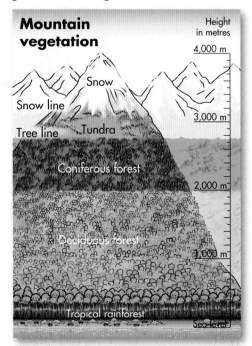

Mountain vegetation

Height in metres

4,000 m
Snow
Snow line
3,000 m
Tree line — Tundra
Coniferous forest
2,000 m
Deciduous forest
1,000 m
Tropical rainforest
Sea-level

Tundra
Long, dry, cold winters. Grasses, moss, bog and dwarf trees.

Cold desert
Very cold with little rain or snow. No plants can grow.

Coniferous forest
Harsh winters, mild summers. Trees have leaves all year.

Deciduous forest
Rain all year, cool winters. Trees shed leaves in winter.

Mediterranean
Hot, dry summers. Mild wet winters. Plants adapt to the heat.

Steppe
Some rain with a dry season. Grasslands with some trees.

Desert
Rain is rare. Plants only grow at oases with underground water.

Semi-desert
Poor rains, sparse vegetation. Grass with a few small trees.

Tropical rainforest (jungle)
Very hot and wet all the year. Tall trees and lush vegetation.

Savanna
Mainly dry, but lush grass grows when the rains come.

Tundra

Pingo (mound)

Thin, stony soil with permafrost below

Mosses, lichens and herbs

Cold desert

No plants can grow

Coniferous forest

Evergreen conifers (spruces and firs)

Young tree saplings and small shrubs

Carpet of pine needles

Ferns and brambles on edge of forest

Yearly cycle of a deciduous forest

Spring

Summer

Autumn

Winter

Mediterranean

Small stunted trees

Scrub

Steppe

There are many plants in the steppe grasslands.

People planting crops damages the natural habitat.

Tropical rainforest

Scattered trees with umbrella-shaped tops grow the highest.

Main layer of tall trees growing close together.

Creepers grow up the trees to reach the sunlight.

Ferns, mosses and small plants grow closest to the ground.

Desert

Cactus

Sand blown into dunes by the wind

Palm trees

Oasis

Semi-desert

Joshua trees

Grass and bush

Savanna

Dry season

Wet season

Agriculture, forests and fishing

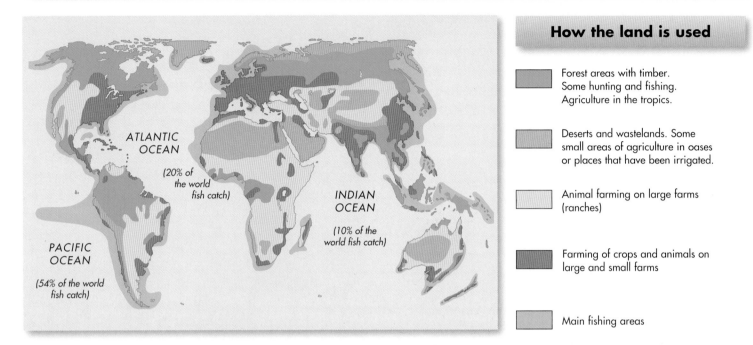

ATLANTIC OCEAN
(20% of the world fish catch)

INDIAN OCEAN
(10% of the world fish catch)

PACIFIC OCEAN
(54% of the world fish catch)

How the land is used

Forest areas with timber. Some hunting and fishing. Agriculture in the tropics.

Deserts and wastelands. Some small areas of agriculture in oases or places that have been irrigated.

Animal farming on large farms (ranches)

Farming of crops and animals on large and small farms

Main fishing areas

The importance of agriculture

Over half the people work in agriculture

Between a quarter and half the people work in agriculture

Between one in ten and a quarter of the people work in agriculture

Less than one in ten of the people work in agriculture

● Countries which depend on agriculture for over half their income

A hundred years ago about 80% of the world's population worked in agriculture. Today it is only about 40% but agriculture is still very important in some countries.

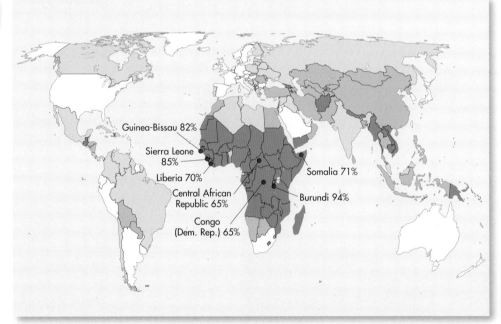

Guinea-Bissau 82%

Sierra Leone 85%

Liberia 70%

Central African Republic 65%

Congo (Dem. Rep.) 65%

Somalia 71%

Burundi 94%

Methods of fishing

There are two types of sea fishing:

1. **Deep-sea fishing** using large trawlers which often stay at sea for many weeks.

2. **Inshore fishing** using small boats, traps and nets up to 70 km from the coast.

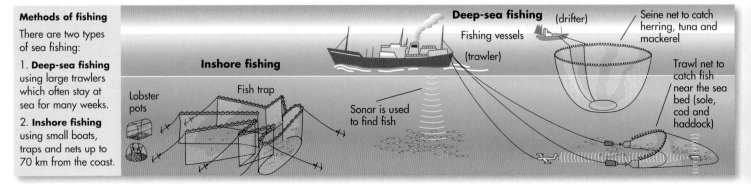

Inshore fishing

Lobster pots

Fish trap

Sonar is used to find fish

Deep-sea fishing (drifter)

Fishing vessels

(trawler)

Seine net to catch herring, tuna and mackerel

Trawl net to catch fish near the sea bed (sole, cod and haddock)

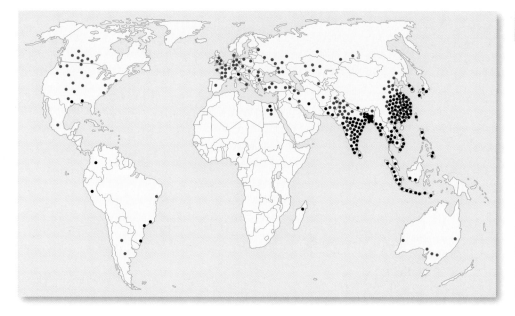

Wheat and rice

- One dot stands for 4 million tonnes of wheat produced
- One dot stands for 4 million tonnes of rice produced

Wheat is the main cereal crop grown in cooler regions. Rice is the main food for over half the people in the world. It is grown in water in paddy fields in tropical areas. Nearly a third of the world's rice is grown in China.

Cattle and sheep

- One dot stands for 10 million cattle
- One dot stands for 10 million sheep

Meat, milk and leather come from cattle. The map shows that they are kept in most parts of the world except where it is hot or very cold. Sheep are kept in cooler regions and they can live on poorer grassland than cows. Sheep are reared for meat and wool.

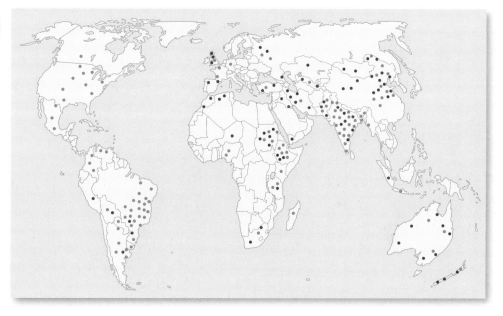

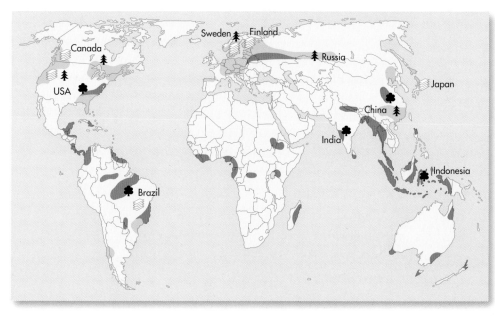

Timber

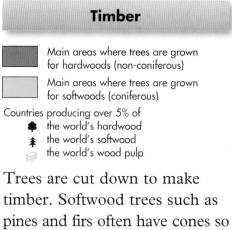

Main areas where trees are grown for hardwoods (non-coniferous)

Main areas where trees are grown for softwoods (coniferous)

Countries producing over 5% of
- ♣ the world's hardwood
- ♠ the world's softwood
- ≋ the world's wood pulp

Trees are cut down to make timber. Softwood trees such as pines and firs often have cones so they are called coniferous. Some trees are chopped up into wood pulp which is used to make paper.

Minerals and energy

Important metals

- ■ Iron ore
- ▲ Bauxite
- ● Copper

Iron is the most important metal in manufacturing. It is mixed with other metals to make steel which is used for ships, cars and machinery. Bauxite ore is used to make aluminium. Aluminium is light and strong. It is used to make aeroplanes. Copper is used for electric wires, and also to make brass and bronze.

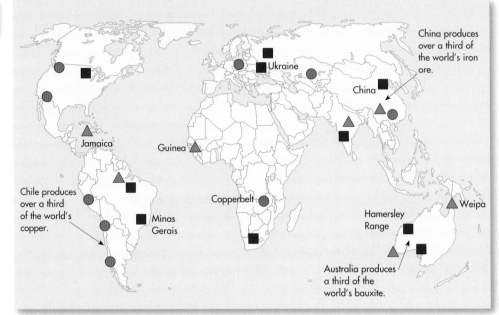

China produces over a third of the world's iron ore.

Ukraine

China

Jamaica

Guinea

Chile produces over a third of the world's copper.

Copperbelt

Minas Gerais

Weipa

Hamersley Range

Australia produces a third of the world's bauxite.

Precious metals and minerals

- Gold
- ★ Silver
- ♦ Diamonds

Some minerals like gold, silver and diamonds are used to make jewellery. They are also important in industry. Diamonds are the hardest mineral and so they are used on tools that cut or grind. Silver is used in photography to coat film, and to make electrical goods. Gold is used in the electronics industry.

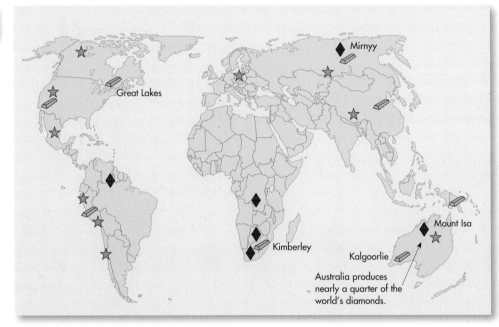

Mirnyy

Great Lakes

Mount Isa

Kimberley

Kalgoorlie

Australia produces nearly a quarter of the world's diamonds.

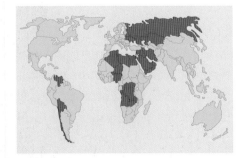

There are over 70 different types of metals and minerals in the world. The maps above show the main countries where some of the most important ones are mined. After mining, metals and fuels are often exported to other countries where they are manufactured into goods. The map on the left shows which countries depend most on mining for their exports and wealth. These countries are coloured red.

Oil and gas

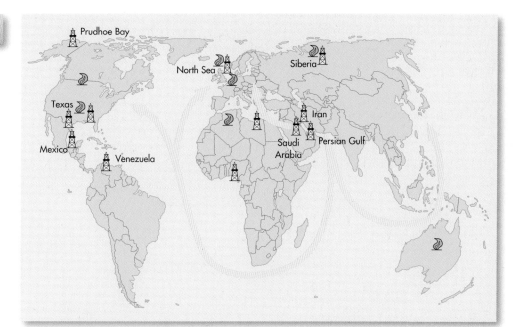

Oilfields

Natural gasfields

Main routes for transporting oil and gas by tanker

Crude oil is drilled from deep in the Earth's crust. The oil is then refined so that it can be used in different industries. Oil is used to make petrol and is also very important in the chemical industry. Natural gas is often found in the same places as oil.

Coal

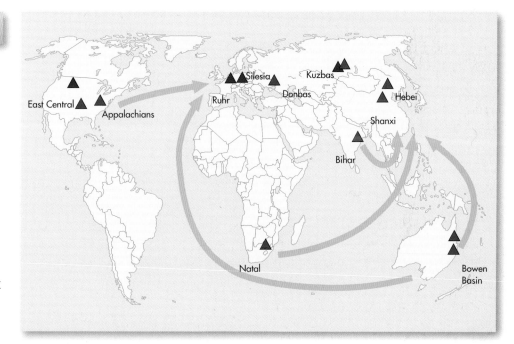

▲ Lignite (soft brown coal)

▲ Hard coal (bituminous)

Main routes for transporting coal

Coal is a fuel that comes from forests and swamps that rotted millions of years ago and have been crushed by layers of rock. The coal is cut out of the rock from deep mines and also from open-cast mines where the coal is nearer the surface. The oldest type of coal is hard. The coal formed more recently is softer.

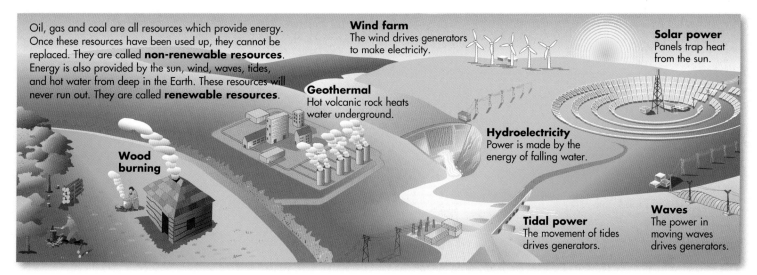

Oil, gas and coal are all resources which provide energy. Once these resources have been used up, they cannot be replaced. They are called **non-renewable resources**. Energy is also provided by the sun, wind, waves, tides, and hot water from deep in the Earth. These resources will never run out. They are called **renewable resources**.

Wind farm
The wind drives generators to make electricity.

Solar power
Panels trap heat from the sun.

Geothermal
Hot volcanic rock heats water underground.

Hydroelectricity
Power is made by the energy of falling water.

Wood burning

Tidal power
The movement of tides drives generators.

Waves
The power in moving waves drives generators.

Peoples and cities of the World

Where people live

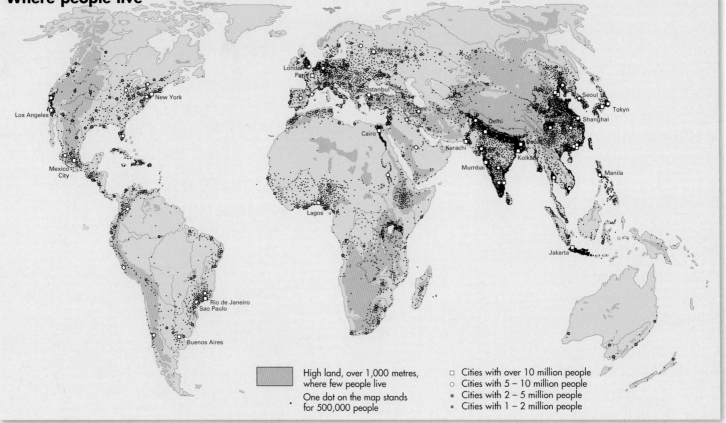

High land, over 1,000 metres, where few people live

. One dot on the map stands for 500,000 people

□ Cities with over 10 million people
○ Cities with 5 – 10 million people
• Cities with 2 – 5 million people
· Cities with 1 – 2 million people

The growth of the population of the world 1000 – 2011 AD

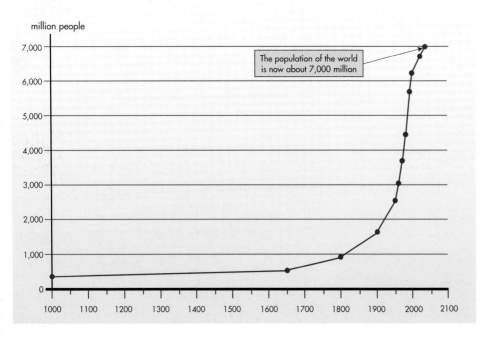

million people

The population of the world is now about 7,000 million

The population of the continents (2010)

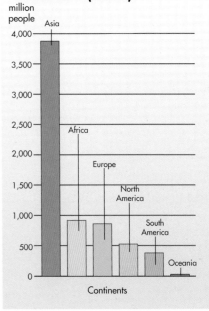

million people

Continents

Population by continents

In this diagram the size of each continent is in proportion to its population. Each square represents 10 million people.

Population of countries in millions

China	1,330
India	1,173
USA	310
Indonesia	243
Brazil	201
Pakistan	184
Bangladesh	156
Nigeria	152
Russia	139
Japan	127
Mexico	112
Philippines	100
Vietnam	90
Ethiopia	88
Germany	82
Egypt	80
Turkey	78
Iran	77
Congo (Dem. Rep.)	71
Thailand	67

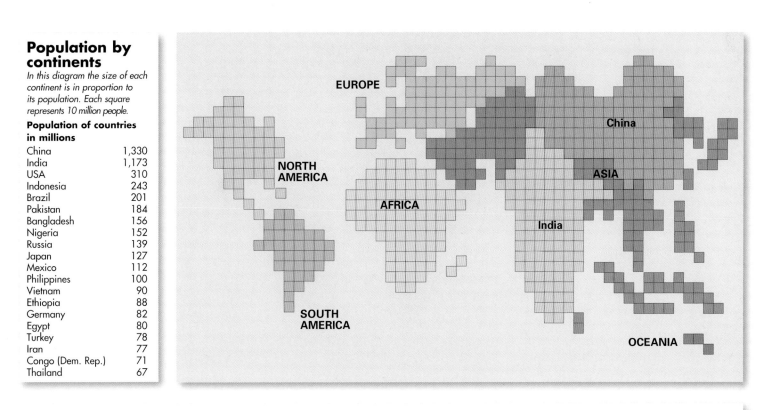

Cities of the World

More people live in cities and towns than in the countryside. These maps show four of the world's largest cities.

- Built-up area – houses, shops and factories
- Poor housing – slums
- City centre – big shops, offices and government buildings
- Parks and woodland
- ● Favelas – areas of poor housing in Rio de Janeiro
- ✈ International airport
- — Major roads

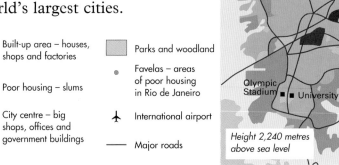

Mexico City
Population 19 million

Texcoco Lake

Zoo
Benito Juarez Airport

Olympic Stadium
University

Height 2,240 metres above sea level

10 kilometres

Shanghai
Population 16 million

Yangtze River

Wusong

Nanxi'ang

Wusong River

Tomb of Lu Xun

The Bund
Pudong New Area

People's Park

Yuyuan Garden

Zoo

Huangpu River

10 kilometres

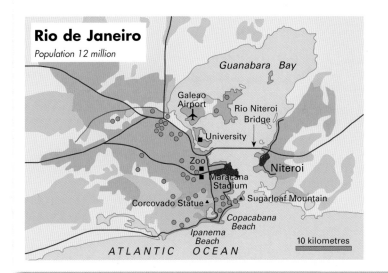

Rio de Janeiro
Population 12 million

Guanabara Bay

Galeao Airport

Rio Niteroi Bridge

University

Zoo

Niteroi

Maracana Stadium

Corcovado Statue

Sugarloaf Mountain

Copacabana Beach

Ipanema Beach

ATLANTIC OCEAN

10 kilometres

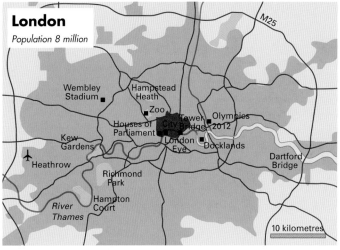

London
Population 8 million

M25

Wembley Stadium
Hampstead Heath
Zoo

Houses of Parliament

Tower Bridge
Olympics 2012

Kew Gardens

London Eye

Docklands

Heathrow

Richmond Park

Dartford Bridge

Hampton Court

River Thames

10 kilometres

Transport and communication

Seaways

—— Main shipping routes

■ The biggest seaports in the world (over a hundred million tonnes of cargo handled a year)

● Other big seaports

Ice and icebergs in the sea all the time, or for some part of the year

—— Large ships can sail on these rivers

Sea transport is used for goods that are too bulky or heavy to go by air. The main shipping routes are between North America, Europe and the Far East.

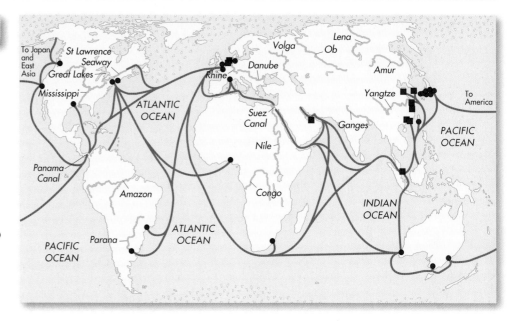

The Panama Canal

Opened in 1914
82 km long
14,000 ships a year

The Suez Canal

Opened in 1870
162 km long
18,000 ships a year

These two important canals cut through narrow pieces of land. Can you work out how much shorter the journeys are by using the canals?

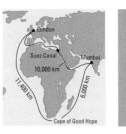

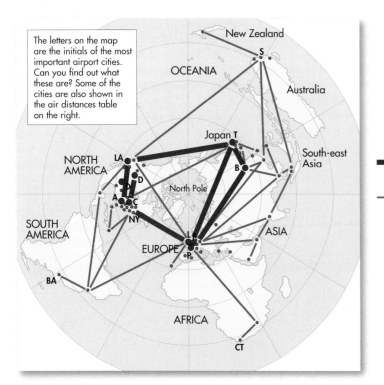

The letters on the map are the initials of the most important airport cities. Can you find out what these are? Some of the cities are also shown in the air distances table on the right.

● Large international airports (over 50 million passengers a year)

· Other important airports

—— Heavily used air routes

—— Other important air routes

Airways

This map has the North Pole at its centre. It shows how much air traffic connects Europe, North America, Japan and Eastern Asia. You can see the long distances in the USA and Russia that are covered by air.

Air distances (kilometres)

	Buenos Aires	Cape Town	London	Los Angeles	New York	Sydney	Tokyo
Buenos Aires		6,880	11,128	9,854	8,526	11,760	18,338
Cape Town	6,880		9,672	16,067	12,551	10,982	14,710
London	11,128	9,672		8,752	5,535	17,005	9,584
Los Angeles	9,854	16,067	8,752		3,968	12,052	8,806
New York	8,526	12,551	5,535	3,968		16,001	10,869
Sydney	11,760	10,982	17,005	12,052	16,001		7,809
Tokyo	18,338	14,710	9,584	8,806	10,869	7,809	

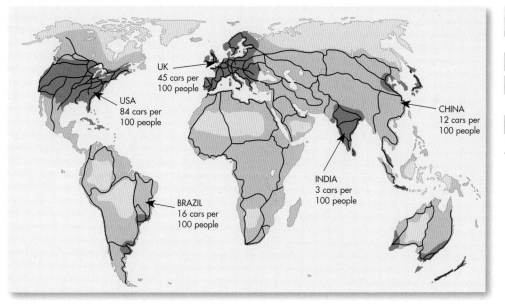

Roads

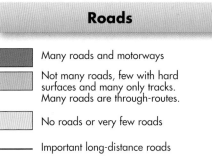

■	Many roads and motorways
▨	Not many roads, few with hard surfaces and many only tracks. Many roads are through-routes.
▧	No roads or very few roads
—	Important long-distance roads

This map shows some of the major roads that link important cities and ports. It also shows how many cars there are in proportion to the number of people in some countries.

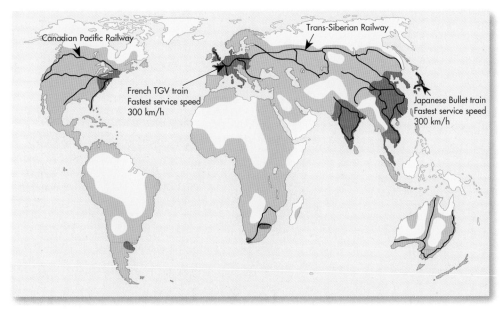

Railways

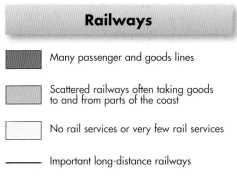

■	Many passenger and goods lines
▨	Scattered railways often taking goods to and from parts of the coast
▢	No rail services or very few rail services
—	Important long-distance railways

This map shows some of the important long-distance railways in the world. Railways are often used for transporting goods between cities and to ports.

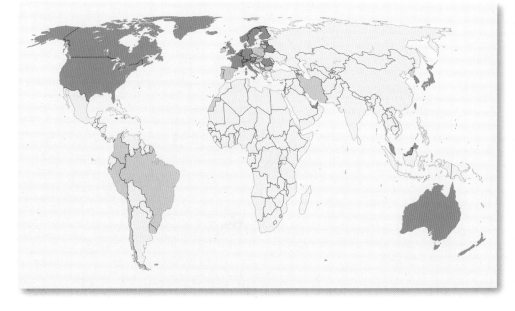

Internet

■	Over half the population use the internet
▨	Between a quarter and a half of the population use the internet
▢	Under a quarter of the population use the internet

The internet started in the 1960s and has now grown into a huge network with nearly 2 billion users around the world. The most popular uses of the internet are email and the world wide web.

43

Global warming

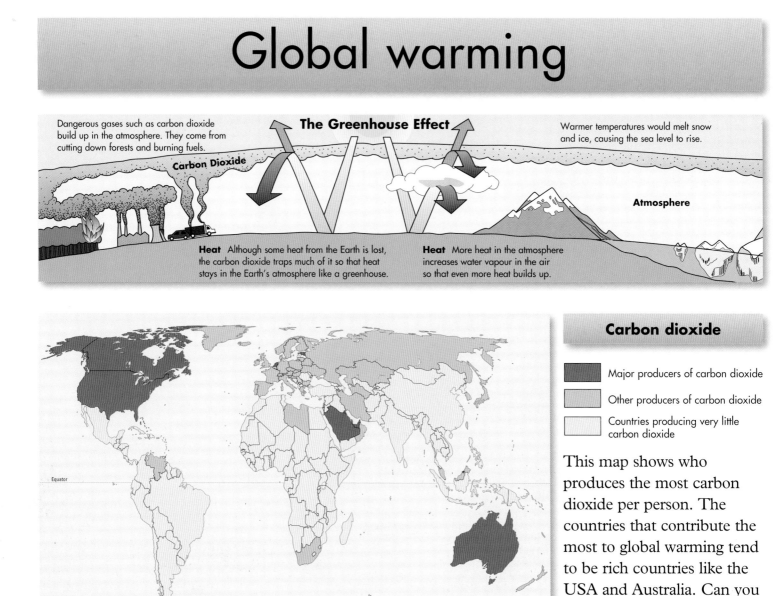

The Greenhouse Effect

Dangerous gases such as carbon dioxide build up in the atmosphere. They come from cutting down forests and burning fuels.

Carbon Dioxide

Warmer temperatures would melt snow and ice, causing the sea level to rise.

Atmosphere

Heat Although some heat from the Earth is lost, the carbon dioxide traps much of it so that heat stays in the Earth's atmosphere like a greenhouse.

Heat More heat in the atmosphere increases water vapour in the air so that even more heat builds up.

Equator

Carbon dioxide

▮ Major producers of carbon dioxide

▮ Other producers of carbon dioxide

☐ Countries producing very little carbon dioxide

This map shows who produces the most carbon dioxide per person. The countries that contribute the most to global warming tend to be rich countries like the USA and Australia. Can you think of reasons why?

Global warming

Experts have studied climate data all around the world. They agreed several years ago that climate change really was happening. Leaders of all the major countries in the world came together in Kyoto in Japan to try and agree on what to do about it. This graph shows how temperatures might not rise as much if countries can cut their carbon dioxide emissions.

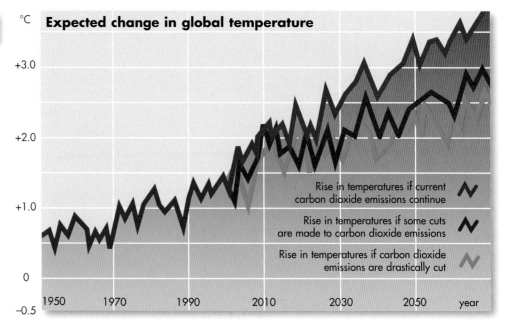

Expected change in global temperature

°C

+3.0

+2.0

+1.0

0

−0.5

1950   1970   1990   2010   2030   2050   year

Rise in temperatures if current carbon dioxide emissions continue

Rise in temperatures if some cuts are made to carbon dioxide emissions

Rise in temperatures if carbon dioxide emissions are drastically cut

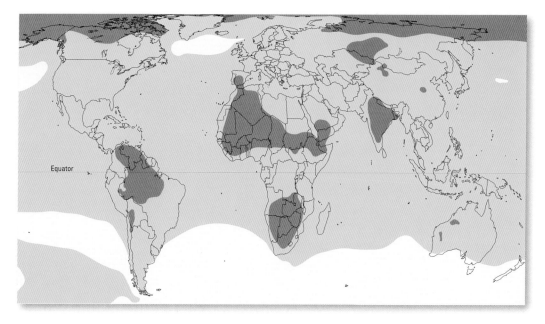

Temperature change

The expected change in temperature in the next 100 years

- More than 5°C warmer
- Betweeen 2°C and 5°C warmer
- Less than 2°C warmer

Compare this map with the map on the opposite page. The countries most affected by temperature change may not be the countries that are causing it.

Rainfall change

The expected change in the amount of rainfall in the next 100 years

- More rainfall
- Very little change in the amount of rainfall
- Less rainfall

As the global climate changes, some parts of the world will get more rainfall, while other parts will become drier. Can you think of the effects this might have?

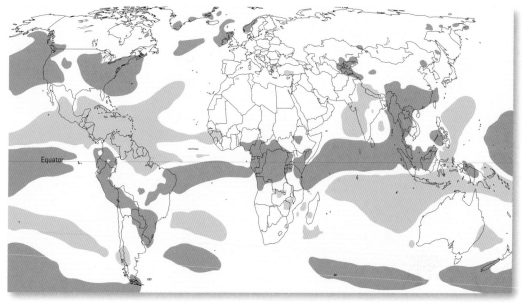

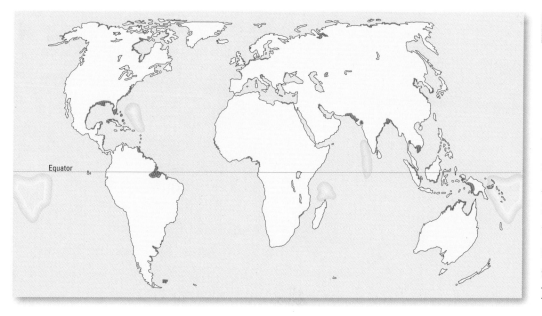

Sea level rise

- Areas at risk from rising sea level
- Areas with many low-lying islands

Warmer temperatures will result in ice caps melting in Antarctica and Greenland. Sea levels will rise and threaten low-lying coastal areas and islands. Some small islands in the Pacific have already disappeared.

45

Rich and poor

All countries have both rich and poor people but some countries have more poor people than others. The amount of food that people have to eat and the age that they die can often depend on where they live in the world. The world can be divided into two parts – the rich and the poor.

The richer countries are mostly in the North and the poorer countries are mostly in the South. The map below shows which countries are rich and which are poor. The list on the right shows some contrasts between rich and poor. Some of these contrasts can be seen in the maps on these pages.

Rich	Poor
Healthy	Poor health
Educated	Poor education
Well fed	Poorly fed
Small families	Large families
Many industries	Few industries
Few farmers	Many farmers
Give aid	Receive aid

The South has over three-quarters of the world's population but less than a quarter of its wealth.

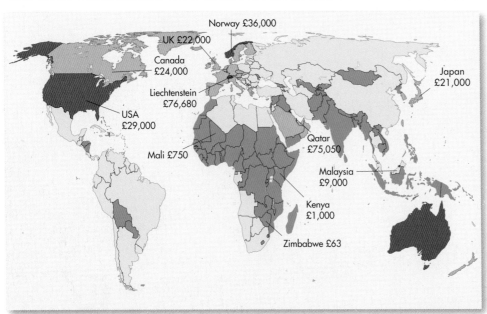

Income

- Very rich countries
- Rich countries
- Poor countries
- Very poor countries

The map shows how much money there is to spend on each person in a country. This is called income per person – this is worked out by dividing the wealth of a country by its population. The map gives examples of rich and poor countries.

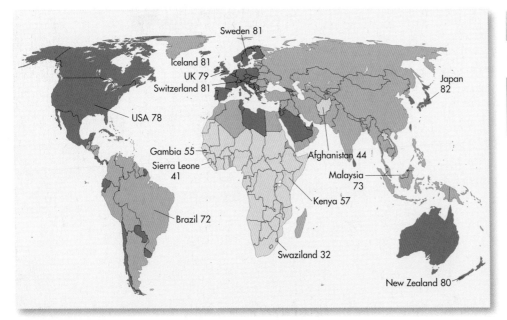

How long do people live?

This is the average age when people die

- Over 75 years
- 60 – 75 years
- Under 60 years

The average age of death is called life expectancy. In the world as a whole, the average life expectancy is 66 years. Some of the highest and lowest ages of death are shown on the map.

Food and famine

☐ Below the amount of food they need

☐ Above the amount of food they need

☐ Over a third above the amount of food they need

★ Major famines since 1980

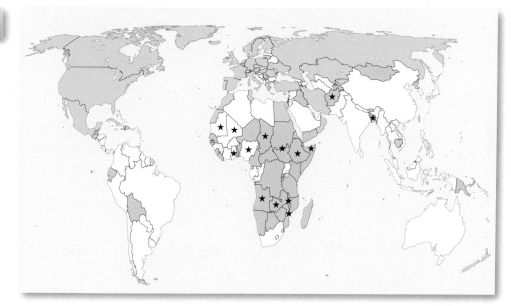

If people do not have enough to eat they become unhealthy. This map shows where in the world people have less than and more than the amount of food they need to live a healthy life.

Reading and writing

☐ Over half the adults cannot read or write

☐ Between a quarter and a half of the adults cannot read or write

☐ Less than a quarter of the adults cannot read or write

The map shows the proportion of adults in each country who cannot read or write a simple sentence. Can you think of some reasons why more people cannot read or write in some places in the world than in others?

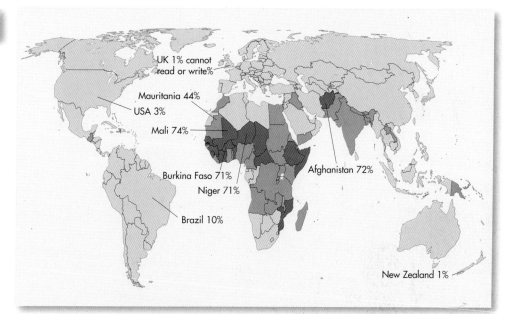

UK 1% cannot read or write%

Mauritania 44%

USA 3%

Mali 74%

Burkina Faso 71%

Niger 71%

Brazil 10%

Afghanistan 72%

New Zealand 1%

Development aid

☐ Over £25 received per person each year

☐ Up to £25 received per person each year

☐ Up to £100 given per person each year

☐ Over £100 given per person each year

☐ Countries that receive or give no aid

Some countries receive aid from other countries. Money is one type of aid. It is used to help with food, health and education problems. The map shows how much different countries give or receive.

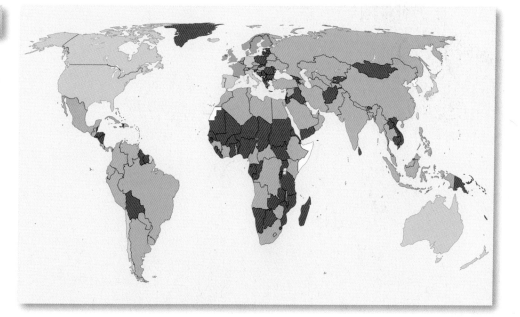

Countries of the World

North America

(see pages 58–59)

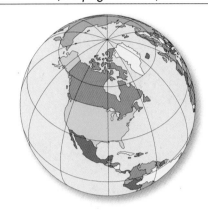

These pages show different maps of the world. The large map shows the world cut through the Pacific Ocean and opened out on to flat paper. The smaller maps of the continents are views of the globe looking down on each of the continents.

Larger maps of the continents appear on the following pages. They show more cities than on this map.

South America

(see pages 60–61)

Africa

(see pages 54–55)

■ Cities with more than 10 million people

48

Europe

(see pages 50–51)

Asia

(see pages 52–53)

Oceania

(see pages 56–57)

REENLAND
(Denmark)

Arctic Circle

ICELAND

Svalbard
(Norway)

40   20   0   20   40   60   80   100   120   140   160   180   80

RUSSIA

60

NORWAY

SWEDEN

FINLAND

UNITED
KINGDOM   DENMARK
IRELAND

ESTONIA
LATVIA
LITHUANIA
BELARUS

■ Moscow

NETH.
GERMANY   POLAND

KAZAKHSTAN

MONGOLIA

■ Paris
FRANCE

BELG.
LUX. CZECH.
AUSTRIA HUNG.
SWITZ. SLO.
CR.
S.
B.-H.
ALB. MAC.

SLOV.
UKRAINE
MOLDOVA
ROMANIA

BULGARIA

■ Beijing

NORTH
KOREA

JAPAN

■ Seoul
SOUTH
KOREA

Tokyo

40

ITALY

GREECE

■ Istanbul
TURKEY

GEORGIA
ARM.
AZER.

UZBEKISTAN

KYRGYZSTAN

TAJIKISTAN

CHINA

Osaka

Shanghai ■

PACIFIC

PORTUGAL   SPAIN

C

Azores
(Portugal)

CYPRUS

LEB.

SYRIA

TURKMENISTAN

ISRAEL

IRAQ
JORDAN

IRAN

AFGHANISTAN

PAKISTAN

Delhi ■

NEPAL

BHUTAN

TAIWAN

20

Tropic of Cancer

Canary Islands
(Spain)

MOROCCO

TUNISIA

Cairo ■

KUWAIT

BAHRAIN

QATAR
U.A.E.

Karachi ■

BANGLA-
DESH

Dacca ■
BURMA
(Myanmar)

NORTHERN
MARIANAS

WESTERN
SAHARA

ALGERIA

LIBYA

EGYPT

SAUDI

Kolkata ■

O C E A N

MAURITANIA

MALI   NIGER

CHAD

SUDAN

ARABIA

OMAN

Mumbai ■

INDIA

LAOS
THAI-
LAND

Manila ■ PHILIPPINES

Guam
(U.S.A.)

MARSHALL
ISLANDS

CAPE
VERDE
LANDS

SENEGAL
GAMBIA
GUINEA
BISSAU GUINEA

BURKINA
FASO

ERITREA

YEMEN

DJIBOUTI

SRI
LANKA

CAMBODIA

VIETNAM

PALAU

FEDERATED STATES
OF MICRONESIA

SIERRA
LEONE
LIBERIA

IVORY
COAST

GHANA

NIGERIA

■ Lagos

CENTRAL
AFRICAN
REP.

SOUTH
SUDAN

ETHIOPIA

SOMALI
REPUBLIC

MALDIVES

BRUNEI

MALAYSIA

EQUATORIAL
GUINEA

CAMEROON

UGANDA

KENYA

SINGAPORE
Sumatra

Borneo

New
Guinea

PAPUA
NEW
GUINEA

SOLOMON
ISLANDS

Equator

GABON

CONGO

Democratic
Republic
of the
CONGO

RWANDA
BURUNDI

INDONESIA

KIRIBATI

Ascencion
(U.K.)

CABINDA

TANZANIA

SEYCHELLES

I N D I A N

Jakarta ■

EAST
TIMOR

TUVALU

ANGOLA

MALAWI

ZAMBIA

COMOROS

Cocos Islands
(Australia)

Christmas
Island
(Australia)

VANUATU

FIJI

St. Helena
(U.K.)

O C E A N

ZIMBABWE

MADAGASCAR

MAURITIUS

New
Caledonia
(France)

20

T L A N T I C

NAMIBIA

MOZAMBIQUE

BOTSWANA

Réunion
(France)

Tropic of Capricorn

O C E A N

SWAZILAND

SOUTH
AFRICA

LESOTHO

AUSTRALIA

Tristan da
Cunha (U.K.)

Prince Edward
Islands
(South Africa)

Crozet Islands
(France)

Kerguelen Islands
(France)

NEW
ZEALAND

40

South Georgia
(U.K.)

S O U T H E R N   O C E A N

60

40   20   0   20   40   60   80   100   120   140   160   180

West from Greenwich   East from Greenwich

Antarctic Circle

A n t a r c t i c a

Europe

Largest countries – by area

(thousand square kilometres)

Russia	17,075
Ukraine	604
France	552
Spain	498

Largest countries – by population

(million people)

Russia	139
Germany	82
France	64
United Kingdom	62

Largest cities

(million people)

Moscow (RUSSIA)	10.5
Istanbul (TURKEY)	10.5
Paris (FRANCE)	10.4
London (UK)	8.6

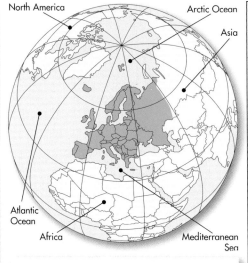

North America · Arctic Ocean · Asia · Atlantic Ocean · Africa · Mediterranean Sea

■ *Europe is the second smallest continent. It is one fifth the size of Asia. Australia is slightly smaller than Europe.*

■ *Great Britain is the largest island in Europe.*

■ *Some people think that the whole of Turkey and Cyprus should be included in Europe.*

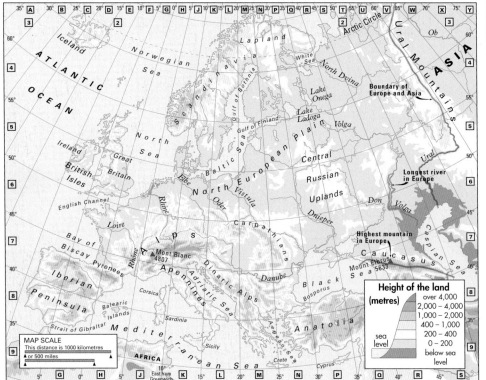

Iceland · ATLANTIC OCEAN · Norwegian Sea · Lapland · White Sea · North Dvina · Ural Mountains · ASIA · Arctic Circle · Ob · Boundary of Europe and Asia · Scandinavia · Gulf of Bothnia · Gulf of Finland · Lake Onega · Lake Ladoga · Volga · North European Plain · Central Russian Uplands · Ural · Longest river in Europe · North Sea · Ireland · Great Britain · British Isles · English Channel · Elbe · Oder · Vistula · Rhine · Don · Dnieper · Volga · Bay of Biscay · Pyrenees · Loire · Alps · Mont Blanc 4807 · Carpathians · Caspian Sea · Danube · Caucasus · Highest mountain in Europe · Mount Elbrus 5633 · Iberian Peninsula · Apennines · Dinaric Alps · Adriatic Sea · Corsica · Black Sea · Bosporus · Balearic Islands · Sardinia · Strait of Gibraltar · Mediterranean Sea · Sicily · Anatolia · Crete · Cyprus · AFRICA · East from Greenwich

MAP SCALE
This distance is 1000 kilometres
or 500 miles

Height of the land
(metres)

	over 4,000
	2,000 – 4,000
	1,000 – 2,000
	400 – 1,000
	200 – 400
sea level	0 – 200
	below sea level

ICELAND · Reykjavik · Faroe Islands (Denmark) · ATLANTIC OCEAN · Orkney Islands · Hebrides · SCOTLAND · Edinbur... · Belfast · IRELAND · Dublin · UNITED KINGDO... · Manche... · WALES · Birmingh... · Cardiff · ENGLA... · London · English Channel · Paris · Nantes · Loire · FRAN... · Bay of Biscay · Bordeaux · Oporto · Bilbao · Lisbon · PORTUGAL · SPAIN · ANDORRA · Madrid · Barcelo... · Valencia · Balearic Islan... · Granada · Maj... · Gibraltar (U.K) · Strait of Gibraltar · Palma · Ceuta (Spain) · Melilla (Spain) · Me... · AFRIC... · West from Greenwich · East from Greenwich

ARCTIC OCEAN

North Cape

North
Sea

Shetland
Islands
(U.K.)

Lofoten
Islands

Arctic Circle

Narvik

Trondheim

Bergen

Oslo

Gothenburg

Stockholm

Copenhagen

DENMARK

Hamburg

Amsterdam

The Hague

HERLANDS

ssels

ELGIUM

GERMANY

Berlin

Frankfurt

LUXEMBOURG

Luxembourg

Munich

Bern

SWITZERLAND

LIECHTENSTEIN

AUSTRIA

Vienna

Milan

Turin

MONACO

seilles

rsica
rance)

nia

Rome

Naples

Palermo

Sicily

rranean
Sea

MALTA

Valletta

Murmansk

White
Sea

Arkhangelsk

North Dvina

Lake Onega

Perm

Lake Ladoga

Helsinki

St. Petersburg

FINLAND

Gulf of Bothnia

Gulf of Finland

Tallinn

ESTONIA

Riga

LATVIA

LITHUANIA

Vilnius

Minsk

BELARUS

Baltic Sea

KALININGRAD
(Russia)

Gdansk

POLAND

Warsaw

Krakow

CZECH
REPUBLIC

Prague

Oder

Elbe

Rhine

Visttula

B

SLOVAK
REPUBLIC

Bratislava

Budapest

HUNGARY

Ljubljana

SLOVENIA

Zagreb

CROATIA

BOSNIA
HERZEGOVIN
A

Sarajevo

SERBIA

Belgrade

MONTENEGRO

Podgorica

KOSOVO

Pristina

MACEDONIA

Skopje

Tirane

Adriatic Sea

SAN
MARINO

RUSSIA

Moscow

Kazan

Samara

Voronezh

Volgograd

Don

Volga

Kiev

Kharkov

UKRAINE

Dnepropetrovsk

Donetsk

Rostov

MOLDOVA

Chisinau

Odessa

ROMANIA

Bucharest

Danube

BULGARIA

Sofia

Sea of
Azov

Crimea

Sevastopol

Black Sea

Krasnodar

Ural

Caspian Sea

Volga

GEORGIA

Tbilisi

ARMENIA

Yerevan

AZERBAIJAN

Baku

NACHICEVAN
(Azerbaijan)

Bosporus

Istanbul

Ankara

TURKEY

GREECE

Aegean Sea

Izmir

Athens

Crete

Nicosia

CYPRUS

ASIA

North

W   E

S

Map information

Cities

Capital city

Index square - see index

Country boundary

Sea and lakes

MAP SCALE

This distance is 750 kilometres

or 500 miles

COPYRIGHT PHILIP'S

Asia

Largest countries – by area
(thousand square kilometres)

Russia	17,075
China	9,597
India	3,287

Largest countries – by population
(million people)

China	1,330
India	1,173
Indonesia	242
Russia	139

Largest cities
(million people)

Tokyo (JAPAN)	36.6
Delhi (INDIA)	22.1
Mumbai (INDIA)	20.0
Shanghai (CHINA)	16.5
Kolkata (INDIA)	15.5

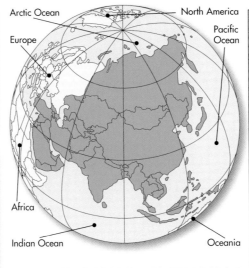

Arctic Ocean · North America · Pacific Ocean · Europe · Africa · Indian Ocean · Oceania

- Asia is the largest continent. It is twice the size of North America.
- It is a continent of long rivers. Many of Asia's rivers are longer than Europe's longest rivers.
- Asia contains well over half the world's population.

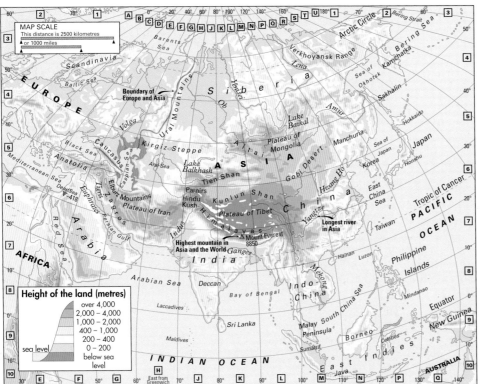

MAP SCALE
This distance is 2500 kilometres
or 1000 miles

Height of the land (metres)

	over 4,000
	2,000 – 4,000
	1,000 – 2,000
	400 – 1,000
	200 – 400
sea level	0 – 200
	below sea level

Map information

- ■● Cities
- ★ Capital city
- Ⓐ Index square – see index
- —— Country boundary
- Sea and lakes

MAP SCALE

This distance is 2000 kilometres

or 1000 miles

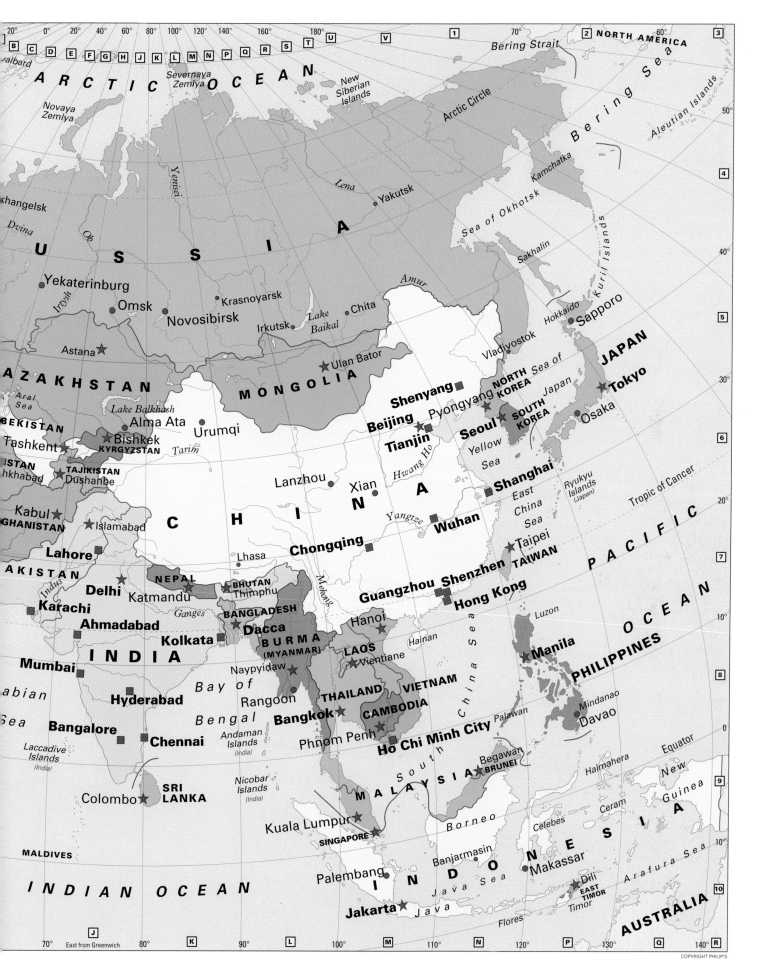

ARCTIC OCEAN

Bering Strait

NORTH AMERICA

Bering Sea

Severnaya Zemlya

New Siberian Islands

Arctic Circle

Aleutian Islands

Novaya Zemlya

Yenisei

Lena

Yakutsk

Sea of Okhotsk

Kamchatka

R U S S I A

Dvina

Yekaterinburg

Ob

Krasnoyarsk

Chita

Kuril Islands

Irtysh

Omsk

Novosibirsk

Irkutsk

Lake Baikal

Sakhalin

Hokkaido

Sapporo

Astana

Vladivostok

Sea of Japan

JAPAN

KAZAKHSTAN

Ulan Bator

M O N G O L I A

Shenyang

Beijing

NORTH KOREA

★Tokyo

Aral Sea

Lake Balkhash

Pyongyang

SOUTH KOREA

Osaka

UZBEKISTAN

Alma Ata

Urumqi

Tianjin

Seoul

Tashkent

Bishkek

KYRGYZSTAN

Tarim

Yellow Sea

KISTAN

TAJIKISTAN

Dushanbe

Lanzhou

Xian

C H I N A

Hwang Ho

Shanghai

East China Sea

Ryukyu Islands (Japan)

Tropic of Cancer

khabad

Kabul

Islamabad

Yangtze

Wuhan

GHANISTAN

C H I N A

Chongqing

Lhasa

NEPAL

BHUTAN

Mekong

Guangzhou Shenzhen

Taipei

TAIWAN

P A C I F I C

Lahore

Katmandu

Thimphu

Hanoi

Hong Kong

AKISTAN

Delhi

BANGLADESH

BURMA (MYANMAR)

LAOS

Luzon

O C E A N

Karachi

Dacca

Vientiane

Ahmadabad

Kolkata

Naypyidaw

THAILAND

VIETNAM

Manila

PHILIPPINES

Mumbai

I N D I A

Hyderabad

Rangoon

Bay of Bengal

Bangkok

CAMBODIA

Mindanao

Davao

Bangalore

Andaman Islands (India)

Phnom Penh

Ho Chi Minh City

Palawan

South China Sea

Equator

abian Sea

Chennai

Laccadive Islands (India)

SRI LANKA

Nicobar Islands (India)

M A L A Y S I A

Begawan

BRUNEI

Halmahera

New Guinea

Ceram

Colombo

Kuala Lumpur

SINGAPORE

Borneo

Celebes

MALDIVES

Banjarmasin

I N D O N E S I A

Makassar

Arafura Sea

I N D I A N   O C E A N

Palembang

Java Sea

Dili

EAST TIMOR

Jakarta

Java

Timor

Flores

AUSTRALIA

East from Greenwich

COPYRIGHT PHILIP'S

53

Africa

- Africa is the second largest continent. Asia is the largest.
- There are over 50 countries, some of them small in area and population. The population of Africa is growing more quickly than any other continent.
- Parts of Africa have a dry, desert climate. Other parts are tropical.
- The highest mountains run from north to south on the eastern side of Africa. The Great Rift Valley is a volcanic valley that was formed 10 to 20 million years ago by a crack in the Earth's crust. Mount Kenya and Mount Kilimanjaro are examples of old volcanoes in the area.
- The Sahara desert is the largest desert in the world.

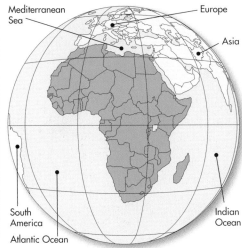

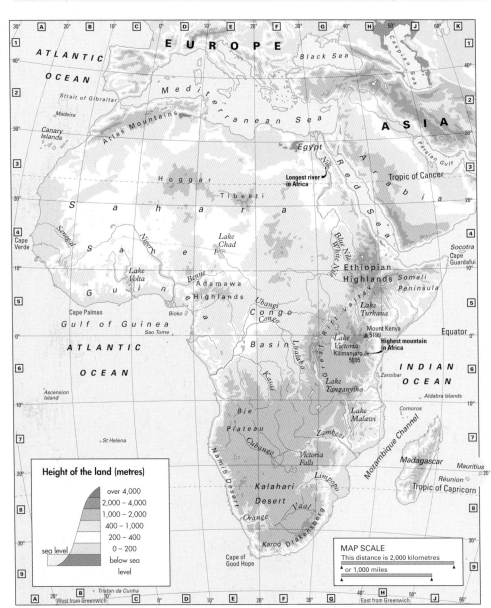

Largest countries – by area

(thousand square kilometres)

Algeria	2,382
Congo (Dem. Rep.)	2,345
Sudan	1,862
Libya	1,760
Chad	1,284
Niger	1,267

Largest countries – by population

(million people)

Nigeria	152
Ethiopia	88
Egypt	80
Congo (Dem. Rep.)	71
South Africa	49
Tanzania	42

Largest cities

(million people)

Cairo (EGYPT)	11.1
Lagos (NIGERIA)	11.1
Kinshasa (CONGO, DEM. REP.)	8.7
Khartoum (SUDAN)	5.1
Luanda (ANGOLA)	4.8

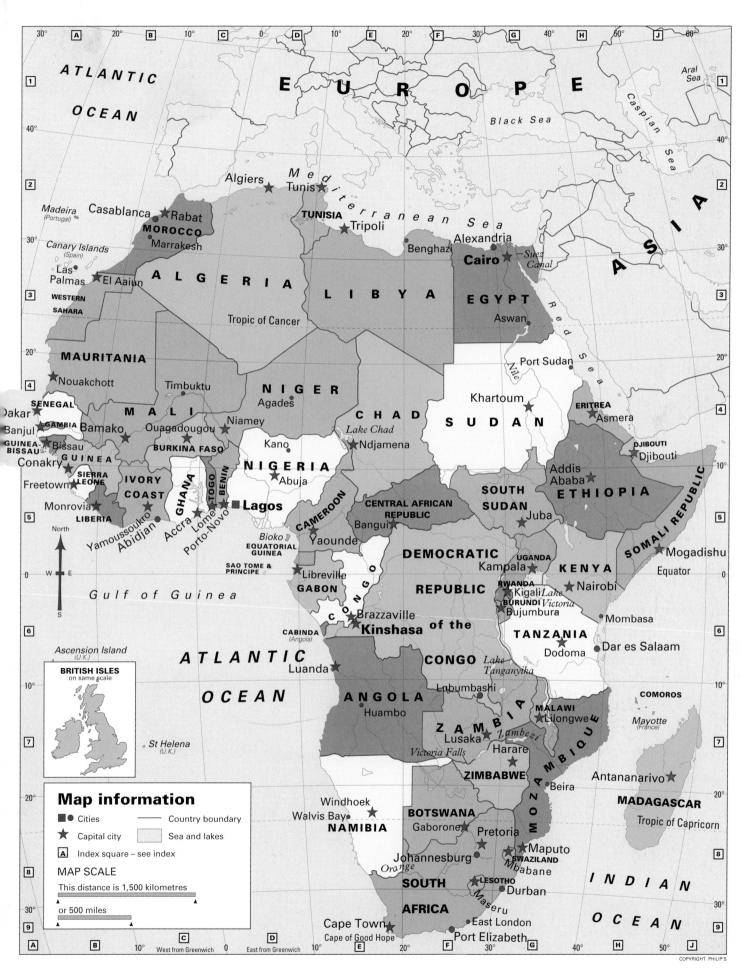

ATLANTIC

OCEAN

E U R O P E

Aral Sea

Black Sea

Caspian Sea

Madeira
(Portugal)

Algiers
Tunis

Mediterranean Sea

Casablanca
Rabat
MOROCCO
Marrakesh

TUNISIA

Tripoli

Benghazi

Alexandria

Cairo

Suez Canal

A S I A

Canary Islands
(Spain)

Las
Palmas
El Aaiun

30°

A L G E R I A

L I B Y A

EGYPT

Aswan

Red Sea

**WESTERN
SAHARA**

Tropic of Cancer

Nile

Port Sudan

MAURITANIA

Nouakchott

Timbuktu

N I G E R

Agades

Khartoum

S U D A N

ERITREA
Asmera

Dakar
SENEGAL

MALI

Niamey

CHAD

Lake Chad

Ndjamena

DJIBOUTI
Djibouti

Banjul
GAMBIA
**GUINEA-
BISSAU**
Bissau

Bamako

Ouagadougou

BURKINA FASO

Kano

Addis
Ababa

ETHIOPIA

Conakry
GUINEA

NIGERIA

Abuja

**SOUTH
SUDAN**

Freetown
**SIERRA
LEONE**

**IVORY
COAST**

Lagos

CAMEROON

**CENTRAL AFRICAN
REPUBLIC**

Juba

SOMALI REPUBLIC

Monrovia
LIBERIA

Yamoussoukro
Abidjan

Accra
Lome
Porto-Novo

GHANA
TOGO
BENIN

Bangui

Yaounde

Bioko
**EQUATORIAL
GUINEA**

DEMOCRATIC

Mogadishu

Equator

North

W E
S

**SAO TOME &
PRINCIPE**

Libreville

GABON

Gulf of Guinea

CONGO

Brazzaville

REPUBLIC

Kampala
UGANDA

KENYA

RWANDA
Kigali
BURUNDI
Bujumbura

*Lake
Victoria*

Nairobi

Mombasa

Kinshasa

of the

CABINDA
(Angola)

CONGO

Luanda

ATLANTIC

OCEAN

*Lake
Tanganyika*

TANZANIA

Dodoma

Dar es Salaam

Ascension Island
(U.K.)

BRITISH ISLES
on same scale

Lubumbashi

ANGOLA

Huambo

COMOROS

MALAWI
Lilongwe

Mayotte
(France)

ZAMBIA

Zambezi

Lusaka

**M
O
Z
A
M
B
I
Q
U
E**

St Helena
(U.K.)

Victoria Falls

Harare

ZIMBABWE

Beira

Antananarivo

Windhoek

BOTSWANA

Walvis Bay

Gaborone

Pretoria

MADAGASCAR

Tropic of Capricorn

Map information

- ■● Cities
- ★ Capital city
- Ⓐ Index square – see index
- —— Country boundary
- ▢ Sea and lakes

MAP SCALE

This distance is 1,500 kilometres

or 500 miles

NAMIBIA

Orange

Johannesburg

Maputo
SWAZILAND
Mbabane

LESOTHO
Maseru

Durban

**SOUTH
AFRICA**

Maseru

East London

I N D I A N

O C E A N

Cape Town
Cape of Good Hope

Port Elizabeth

West from Greenwich

East from Greenwich

COPYRIGHT PHILIP'S

55

Australia and Oceania

- The continent is often called Oceania. It is made up of the huge island of Australia and thousands of other islands in the Pacific Ocean.
- It is the smallest continent, only about a sixth the size of Asia.
- The highest mountain is on the Indonesian part of New Guinea which many consider to be part of Asia.

Largest countries – by area	
(thousand square kilometres)	
Australia	7,741
Papua New Guinea	463
New Zealand	271

Largest countries – by population	
(million people)	
Australia	21
Papua New Guinea	6

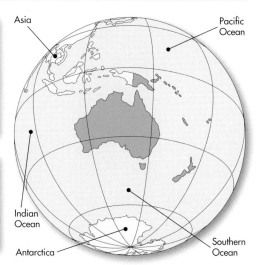

Asia
Pacific Ocean
Indian Ocean
Antarctica
Southern Ocean

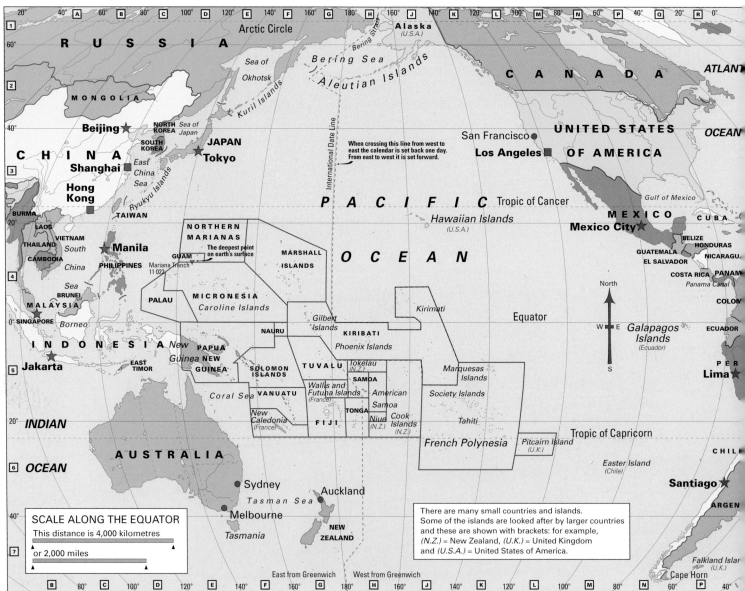

SCALE ALONG THE EQUATOR
This distance is 4,000 kilometres
or 2,000 miles

When crossing this line from west to east the calendar is set back one day. From east to west it is set forward.

There are many small countries and islands. Some of the islands are looked after by larger countries and these are shown with brackets: for example, (N.Z.) = New Zealand, (U.K.) = United Kingdom and (U.S.A.) = United States of America.

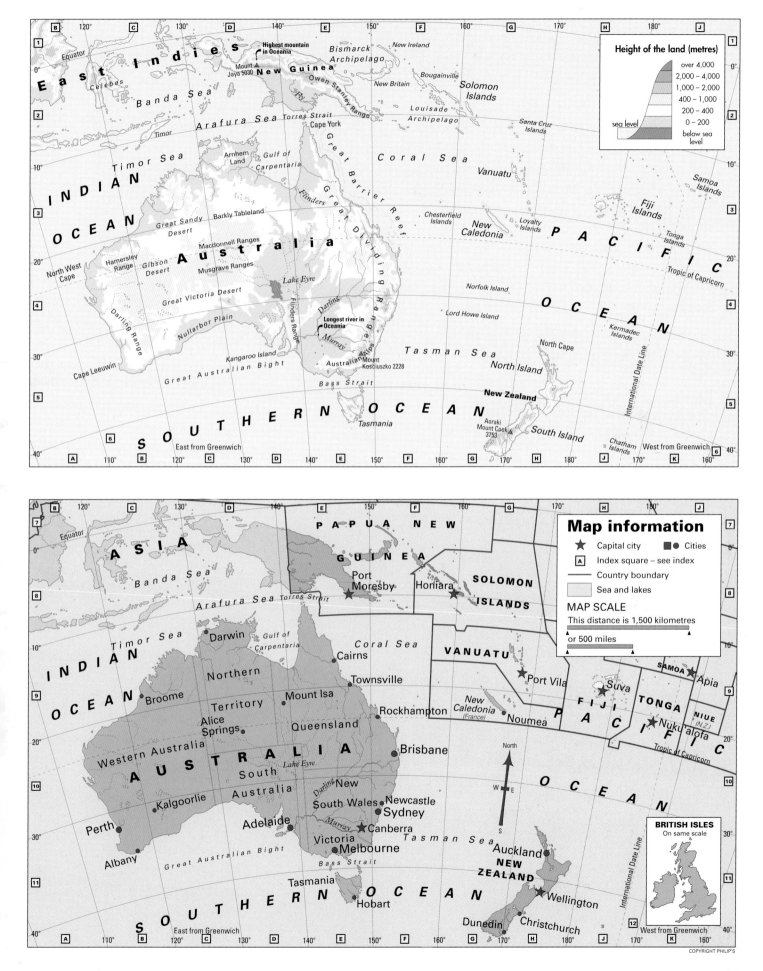

Map 1 (top): Physical map — Australia and Oceania

East Indies

Equator 0°

Celebes

Banda Sea

Timor

Arafura Sea   Torres Strait

INDIAN   Timor Sea

OCEAN

10°

North West Cape

Hamersley Range   Great Sandy Desert   Barkly Tableland

Gibson Desert   Macdonnell Ranges   Australia

20°   Musgrave Ranges

Great Victoria Desert   Lake Eyre

Darling Range   Nullarbor Plain

30°   Cape Leeuwin   Kangaroo Island   Great Australian Bight

Bass Strait

Tasmania

40°   SOUTHERN OCEAN   East from Greenwich

Highest mountain in Oceania

Mount Jaya 5030   New Guinea

Bismarck Archipelago   New Ireland

Owen Stanley Range   New Britain   Bougainville   Solomon Islands

Fly   Louisade Archipelago   Santa Cruz Islands

Cape York   Coral Sea   Vanuatu   Samoa Islands

Great Barrier Reef   Chesterfield Islands   New Caledonia   Loyalty Islands   Fiji Islands

Great Dividing Range   Flinders   PACIFIC   Tonga Islands

Tropic of Capricorn

Flinders Range   Darling   Norfolk Island   Lord Howe Island   OCEAN   Kermadec Islands

Longest river in Oceania   Murray   North Cape   North Island

Australian Alps   Mount Kosciuszko 2228   Tasman Sea   New Zealand

Aoraki Mount Cook 3753   South Island   Chatham Islands   West from Greenwich

Height of the land (metres)
- over 4,000
- 2,000 – 4,000
- 1,000 – 2,000
- 400 – 1,000
- 200 – 400
- sea level 0 – 200
- below sea level

Map 2 (bottom): Political map — Australia and Oceania

Equator

ASIA

Banda Sea

INDIAN   Timor Sea

OCEAN

Arafura Sea   Torres Strait

PAPUA NEW GUINEA

Port Moresby   Honiara   SOLOMON ISLANDS

Darwin   Gulf of Carpentaria   Coral Sea   VANUATU

Broome   Cairns   Port Vila   SAMOA   Apia

Northern Territory   Townsville   FIJI   TONGA

Mount Isa   New Caledonia (France)   Suva   NIUE (N.Z.)

Alice Springs   Queensland   Rockhampton   Noumea   PACIFIC   Nuku'alofa

Western Australia   AUSTRALIA   Brisbane   Tropic of Capricorn

Kalgoorlie   South   Darling New   OCEAN

Perth   Australia   South Wales   Newcastle

Adelaide   Murray   Sydney

Victoria   Canberra   Tasman Sea   Auckland

Albany   Great Australian Bight   Melbourne   NEW ZEALAND

Bass Strait   Wellington

Tasmania   Dunedin   Christchurch

Hobart

SOUTHERN OCEAN   East from Greenwich   West from Greenwich

Map information
- ★ Capital city
- ■ ● Cities
- Ⓐ Index square – see index
- — Country boundary
- Sea and lakes

MAP SCALE

This distance is 1,500 kilometres

or 500 miles

BRITISH ISLES
On same scale

North / W E / S

COPYRIGHT PHILIP'S

57

North America

- North America is the third largest continent. It is half the size of Asia. It stretches almost from the Equator to the North Pole.
- Three countries – Canada, the United States and Mexico – make up most of the continent.
- Greenland, the largest island in the world, is included within North America.

- In the east there are a series of large lakes. These are called the Great Lakes. A large waterfall called Niagara Falls is between Lake Erie and Lake Ontario. The St Lawrence river connects the Great Lakes with the Atlantic Ocean.
- North and South America are joined by a narrow strip of land called the Isthmus of Panama.

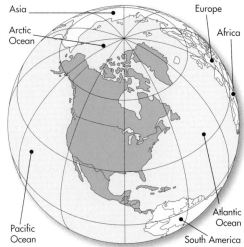

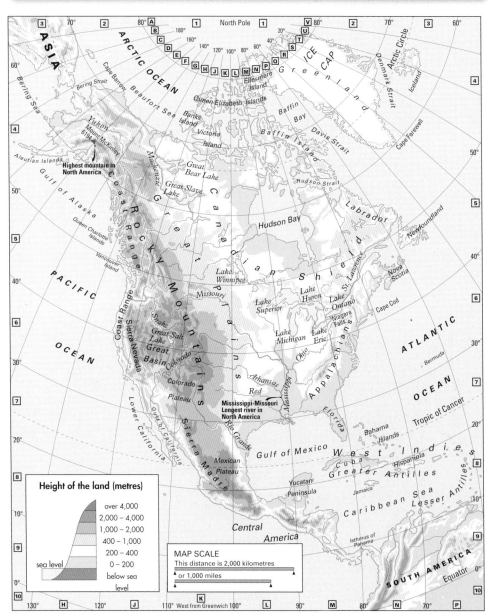

Largest countries – by area

(thousand square kilometres)

Canada	9,971
United States	9,629
Greenland	2,176
Mexico	1,958
Nicaragua	130
Honduras	112

Largest countries – by population

(million people)

United States	310
Mexico	112
Canada	34
Guatemala	13
Cuba	11
Dominican Republic	9

Largest cities

(million people)

Mexico City (MEXICO)	19.4
New York (USA)	19.4
Los Angeles (USA)	12.8
Chicago (USA)	9.2
Miami (USA)	5.7

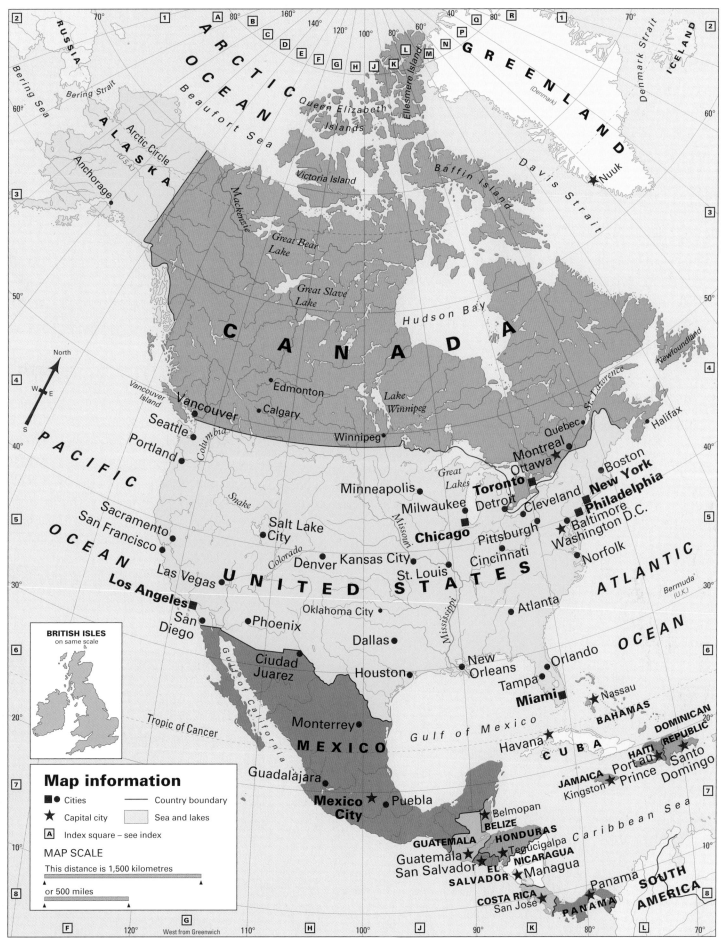

ARCTIC OCEAN

RUSSIA

Bering Sea

Bering Strait

ALASKA (U.S.A.)

Arctic Circle

Anchorage

Beaufort Sea

Queen Elizabeth Islands

Victoria Island

Mackenzie

Ellesmere Island

GREENLAND (Denmark)

Nuuk

Baffin Island

Davis Strait

Denmark Strait

ICELAND

PACIFIC OCEAN

Great Bear Lake

Great Slave Lake

CANADA

Hudson Bay

North

W E
S

Vancouver Island

Vancouver

Seattle

Portland

Edmonton

Calgary

Lake Winnipeg

Winnipeg

Columbia

Newfoundland

St. Lawrence

Quebec

Halifax

Montreal
Ottawa

Boston

New York

Sacramento

San Francisco

Las Vegas

Los Angeles

San Diego

Snake

Salt Lake City

Colorado

Denver

Minneapolis

Milwaukee

Chicago

Missouri

Kansas City

St. Louis

UNITED STATES

Great Lakes

Detroit

Cleveland

Pittsburgh

Cincinnati

Philadelphia

Baltimore
Washington D.C.

Norfolk

ATLANTIC

Bermuda (U.K.)

OCEAN

Phoenix

Oklahoma City

Dallas

Atlanta

Houston

Mississippi

New Orleans

Tampa

Orlando

Miami

Nassau

BAHAMAS

DOMINICAN REPUBLIC

Ciudad Juarez

Gulf of California

Monterrey

MEXICO

Tropic of Cancer

Guadalajara

Mexico City

Puebla

Gulf of Mexico

Havana

CUBA

HAITI

Port au Prince

Santo Domingo

JAMAICA

Kingston

Caribbean Sea

BRITISH ISLES on same scale

Belmopan

BELIZE

GUATEMALA

Guatemala

San Salvador

EL SALVADOR

HONDURAS

Tegucigalpa

NICARAGUA

Managua

Panama

SOUTH AMERICA

COSTA RICA

San Jose

PANAMA

Map information

■ ● Cities

★ Capital city

A Index square – see index

—— Country boundary

Sea and lakes

MAP SCALE

This distance is 1,500 kilometres

or 500 miles

West from Greenwich

COPYRIGHT PHILIP'S

59

South America

- *The Amazon is the second longest river in the world. The Nile is the longest river, but more water flows from the Amazon into the ocean than from any other river.*
- *The range of mountains called the Andes runs for over 7,500 km from north to south on the western side of the continent. There are many volcanoes in the Andes.*

- *Lake Titicaca is the largest lake in the continent. It has an area of 8,300 sq km and is 3,800 metres above sea level.*
- *Spanish and Portuguese are the principal languages spoken in South America.*
- *Brazil is the largest country in area and population and is the richest in the continent.*

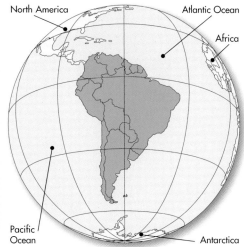

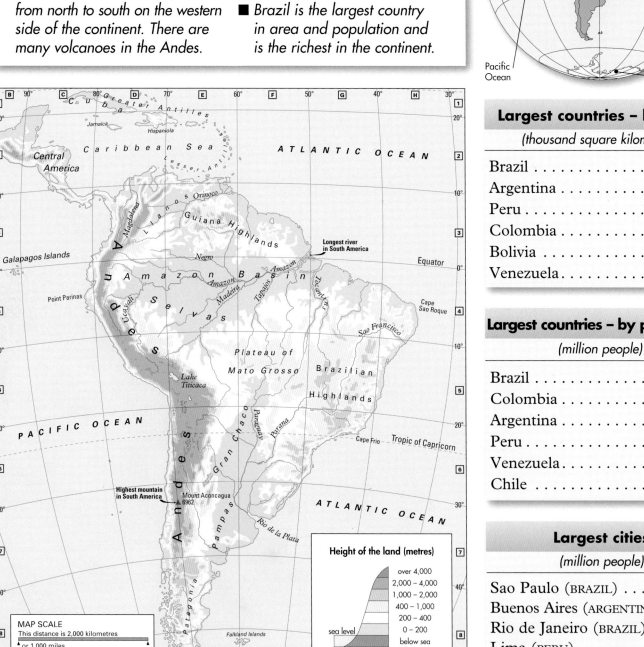

Largest countries – by area

(thousand square kilometres)

Brazil	8,514
Argentina	2,780
Peru	1,285
Colombia	1,139
Bolivia	1,099
Venezuela	912

Largest countries – by population

(million people)

Brazil	201
Colombia	44
Argentina	41
Peru	30
Venezuela	27
Chile	17

Largest cities

(million people)

Sao Paulo (BRAZIL)	20.2
Buenos Aires (ARGENTINA) .	13.3
Rio de Janeiro (BRAZIL) . . .	11.9
Lima (PERU)	8.9
Bogota (COLOMBIA)	7.6

1 B 90° **C** 80° **D** 70° **E** 60° **F** 50° **G** 40° **H** **1**

Havana
C U B A
BAHAMAS
MEXICO
JAMAICA
BELIZE
Kingston
Port au
Prince
Santo
Domingo
DOMINICAN REPUBLIC
HAITI
PUERTO RICO (U.S.A.)
VIRGIN ISLANDS (U.S.A.-U.K.)
ST KITTS-NEVIS
ANTIGUA & BARBUDA
A T L A N T I C
GUATEMALA
HONDURAS
Tegucigalpa
EL SALVADOR
NICARAGUA
Managua
COSTA RICA
San Jose
Panama
PANAMA
Caribbean Sea
Barranquilla
GUADELOUPE (France)
DOMINICA
MARTINIQUE (France)
ST LUCIA
ST VINCENT
BARBADOS
CURAÇAO (Neth.)
GRENADA
Caracas
Port of Spain
TRINIDAD & TOBAGO
O C E A N
Maracaibo
Valencia
VENEZUELA
Orinoco
Georgetown
Paramaribo
Cayenne
GUYANA
SURINAME
FRENCH GUIANA
Medellin
Bogota
C O L O M B I A
Cali
Negro
Amazon
Belem
Equator
Quito
ECUADOR
Galapagos Islands (Ecuador)
Guayaquil
Iquitos
Manaus
Madeira
Tapajos
Fortaleza
Chiclayo
Ucayali
B R A Z I L
Xingu
Tocantins
Sao Francisco
Trujillo
P E R U
Recife
Lima
Cuzco
P A C I F I C
Arequipa
Lake Titicaca
La Paz
Brasilia
Salvador
B O L I V I A
Goiania
Sucre
Belo Horizonte
Antofagasta
PARAGUAY
Sao Paulo
Rio de Janeiro
Parana
Asuncion
Curitiba
Tropic of Capricorn
O C E A N
Tucuman
A T L A N T I C
Porto Alegre
CHILE
Cordoba
Valparaiso
Rosario
URUGUAY
Santiago
Buenos Aires
Montevideo
Rio de la Plata
O C E A N
Concepcion
Juan Fernandez (Chile)
North
W E
S
A R G E N T I N A
Bahia Blanca
BRITISH ISLES
on same scale
Falkland Islands (U.K.)
Stanley
South Georgia (U.K.)
Punta Arenas
Cape Horn

Map information

■ ● Cities
★ Capital city
Ⓐ Index square – see index

—— Country boundary
Sea and lakes

MAP SCALE

This distance is 1,500 kilometres

or 500 miles

COPYRIGHT PHILIP'S

61

Polar Regions

The Polar Regions are the areas around the North Pole and the South Pole. The area around the North Pole is called the **Arctic** and the area around the South Pole is called the **Antarctic**. The sun never shines straight down on the Arctic or Antarctic so they are very cold – the coldest places on Earth. The Arctic consists of frozen water. Some parts of Northern Europe, North America and Asia are inside the Arctic Circle. A group of people called the Inuit live there.

Map information

● Cities and towns

★ Capital cities

● (Japan) Scientific stations in the Antarctic

Land covered in ice

Sea covered in ice

Ice sometimes in the sea

MAP SCALE
This distance is
1,500 kilometres

or 500 miles

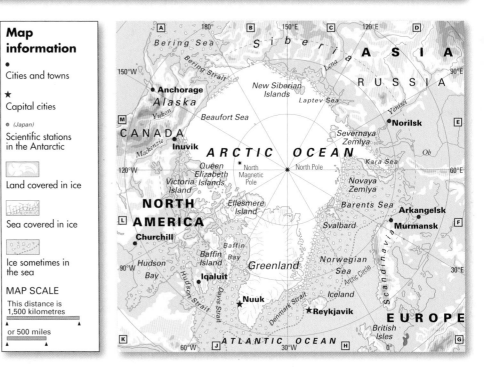

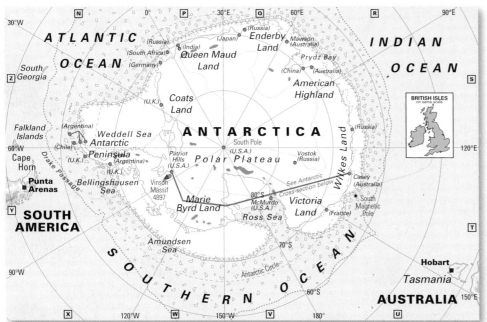

The Antarctic is a continent. It is bigger than Europe or Australia and has no permanent population. Most of the land consists of ice which is thousands of metres thick. At the edges, chunks of ice break off to make icebergs. These float out to sea. The diagram below shows a cross-section through Antarctica between two of the scientific research stations, Patriot Hills and Casey. It shows how thick the ice is on the ice sheets.

Cross-section of the Antarctic

2,000 m — Transantarctic Mountains — East Antarctic Ice Sheet — 2,000 m

1,000 m — Patriot Hills — ICE — ICE — Casey — 1,000 m

Bellingshausen Sea — sea level — West Antarctic Ice Sheet — Ross Ice Shelf — Indian Ocean sea level

–1,000 m — –1,000 m

–2,000 m — –2,000 m

ROCK — ROCK

1,000 km — 2,000 km — 3,000 km — 4,000 km — 5,000 km — 6,000 km

UK, Europe and the World

United Nations

The UN is the largest international organization in the world. The headquarters are in New York and 192 countries are members. It was formed in 1945 to help solve world problems and to help keep world peace. The UN sends peacekeeping forces to areas where there are problems.

★ Current peacekeeping forces with the year they were sent

European Union

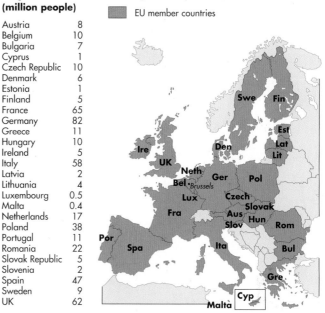

Population (million people)	
Austria	8
Belgium	10
Bulgaria	7
Cyprus	1
Czech Republic	10
Denmark	6
Estonia	1
Finland	5
France	65
Germany	82
Greece	11
Hungary	10
Ireland	5
Italy	58
Latvia	2
Lithuania	4
Luxembourg	0.5
Malta	0.4
Netherlands	17
Poland	38
Portugal	11
Romania	22
Slovak Republic	5
Slovenia	2
Spain	47
Sweden	9
UK	62

EU member countries

The EU was first formed in 1951. Six countries were members. Now there are 27 countries in the EU. These countries meet to discuss agriculture, industry and trade as well as social and political issues. The headquarters are in Brussels. Cyprus, the Czech Republic, Estonia, Hungary, Latvia, Lithuania, Malta, Poland, the Slovak Republic and Slovenia joined the EU in 2004. Bulgaria and Romania joined in 2007.

The Commonwealth

Commonwealth member countries

The Commonwealth is a group of 54 independent countries which used to belong to the British Empire. It is organized by a group of people called the Secretariat which is based in London. Queen Elizabeth II is the head of the Commonwealth. About every two years the heads of the different governments meet to discuss world problems. These meetings are held in different countries in the Commonwealth.

Index

The names in the index are in alphabetical order. To find a place on a map in the atlas, first find the name in the index. The first number after the place name is the map page number. After the page number there is a letter and another number. The **letter** shows you the **column** where the place is on the map and the **number** shows you the **row**. If the place name goes across more than one square, the reference is to the square where the name begins.